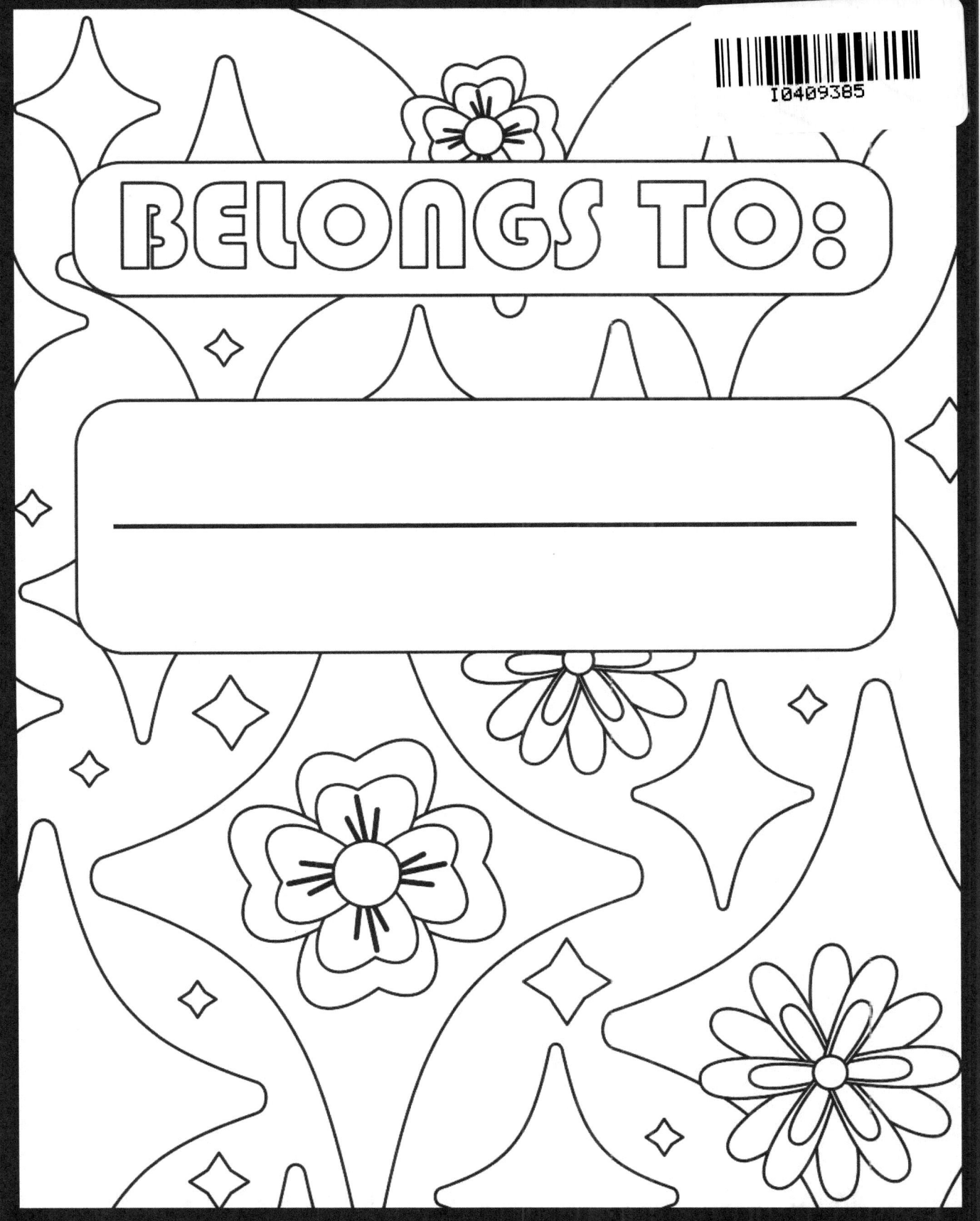

BELONGS TO:

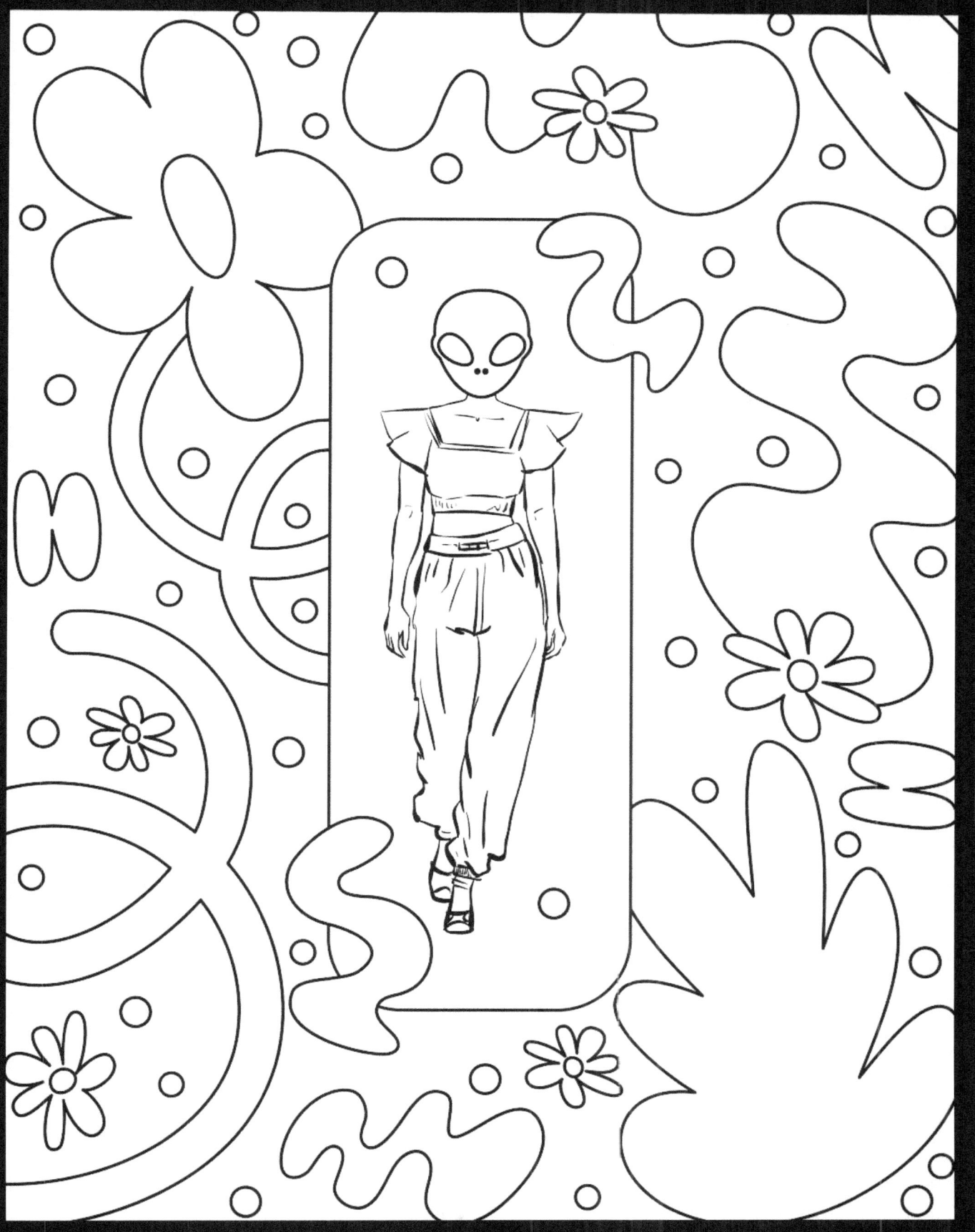

STRUT

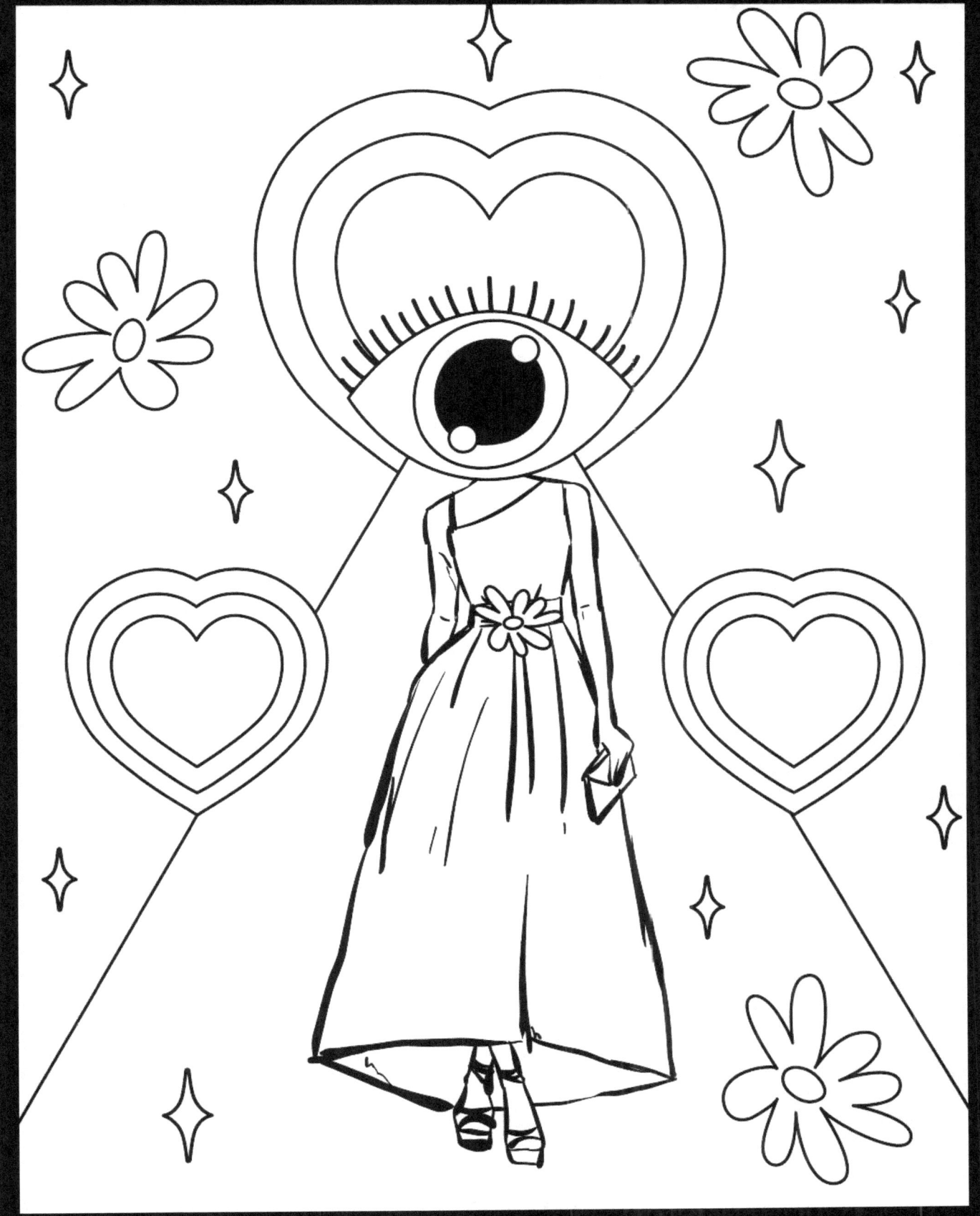

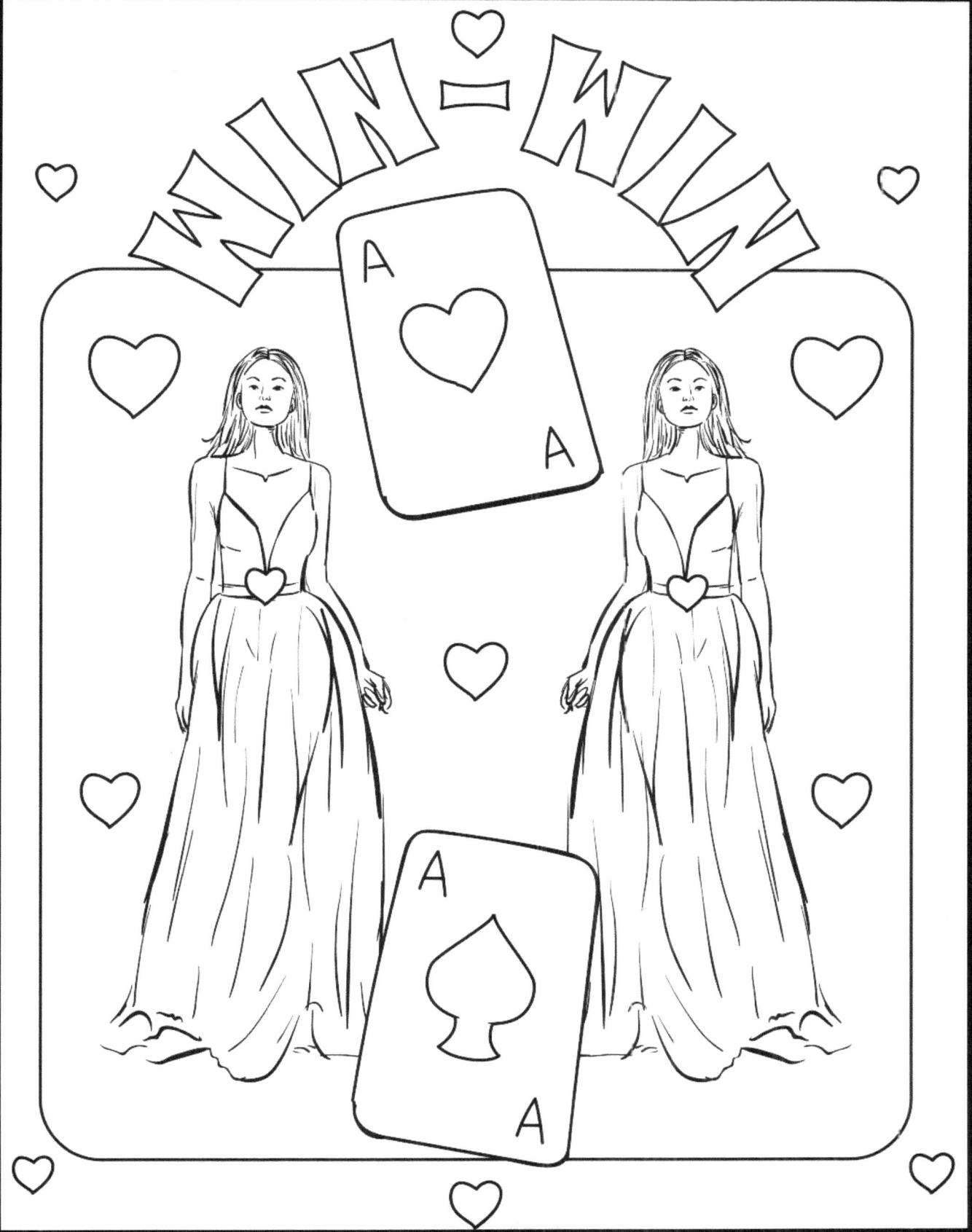

WINNING

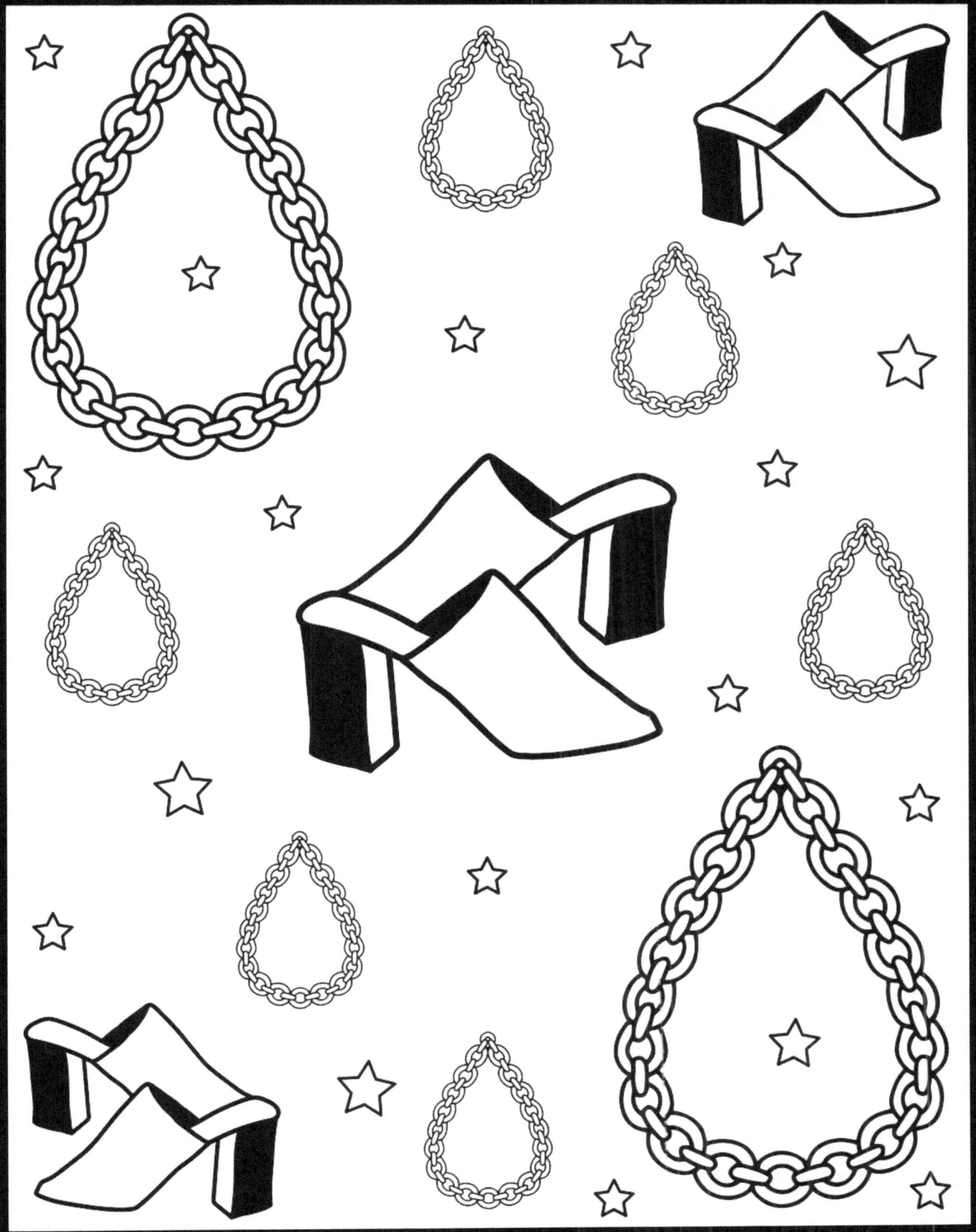

SLIDES

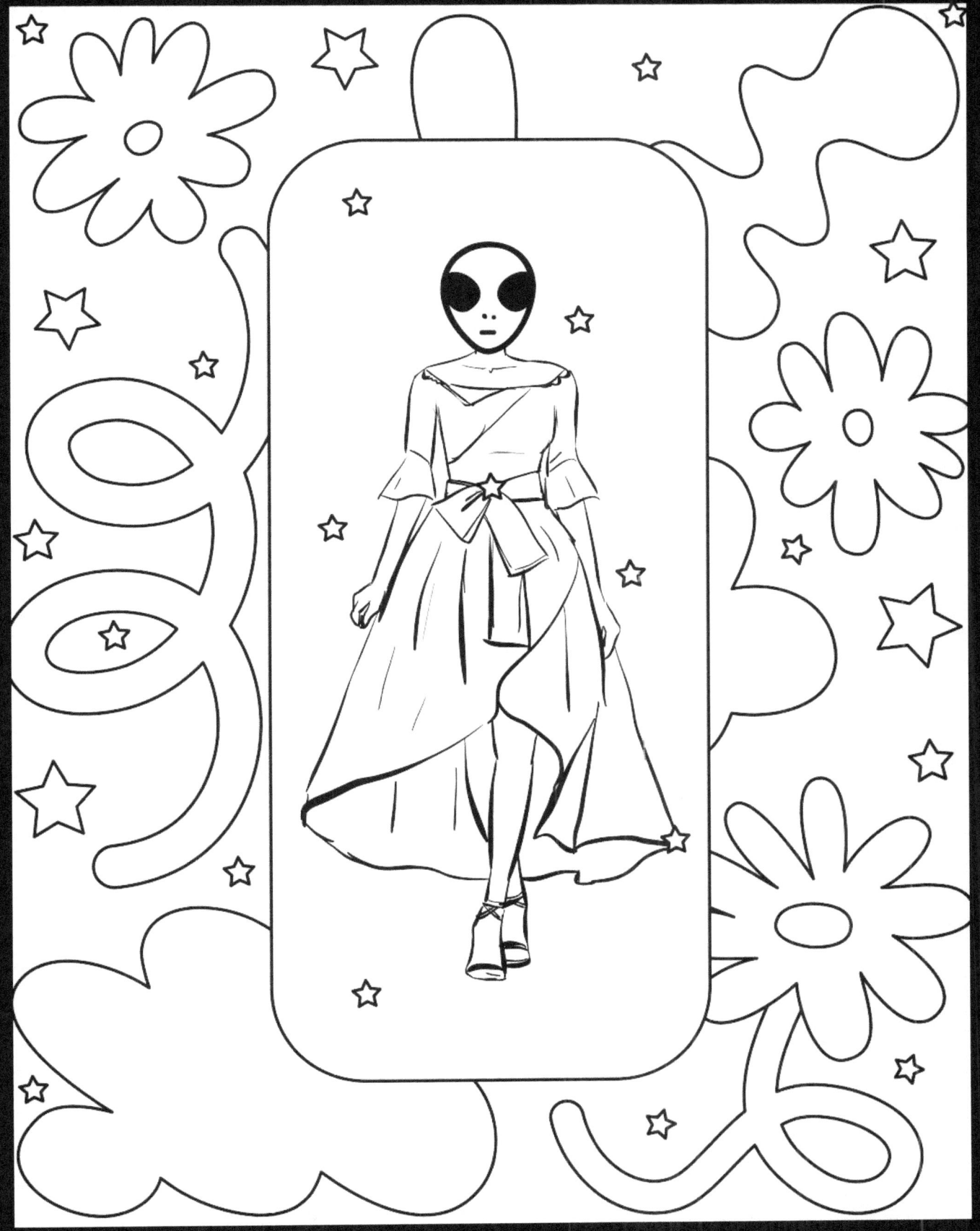

OUT OF THIS WORLD

VIRTUAL

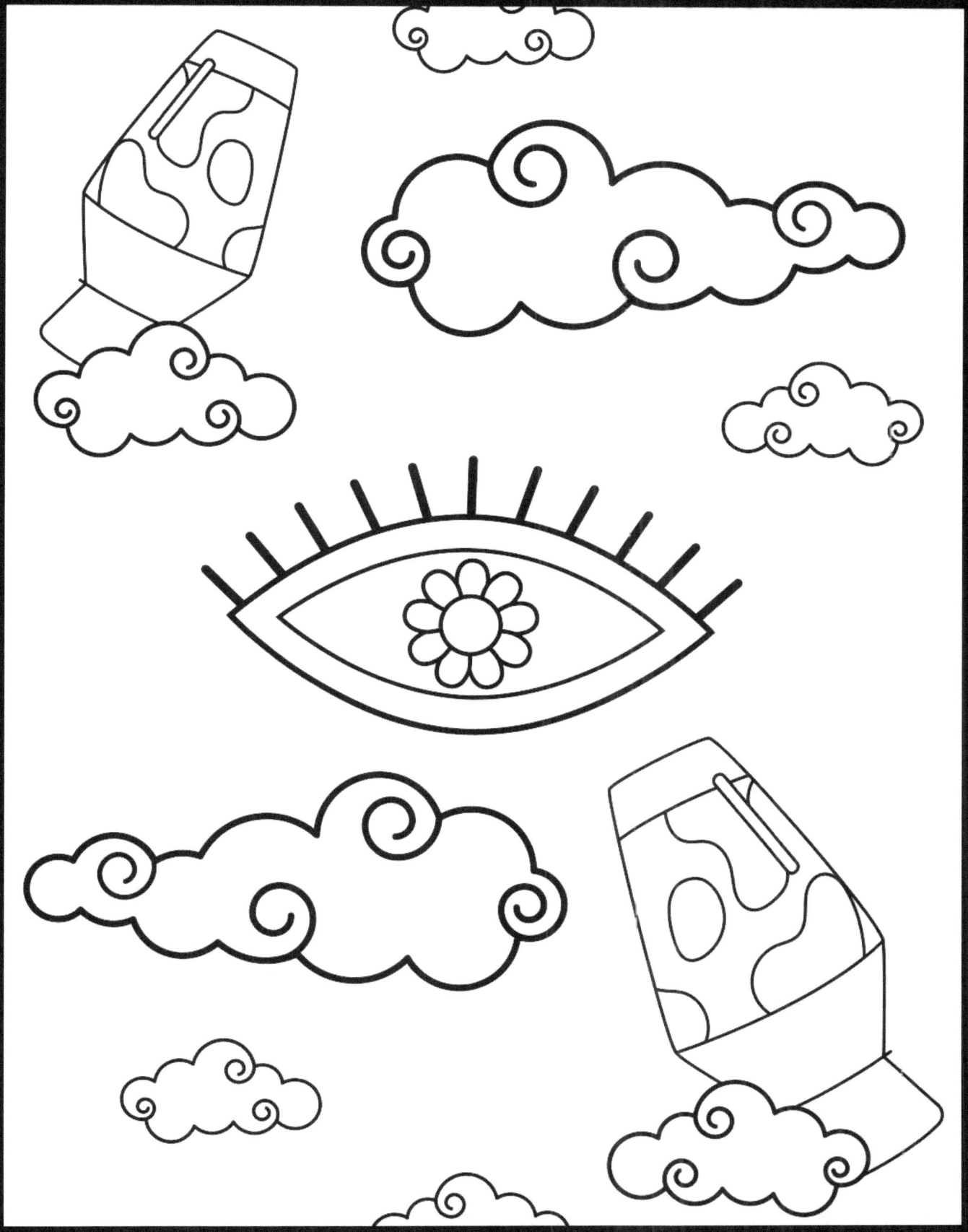

LAVA LOVE

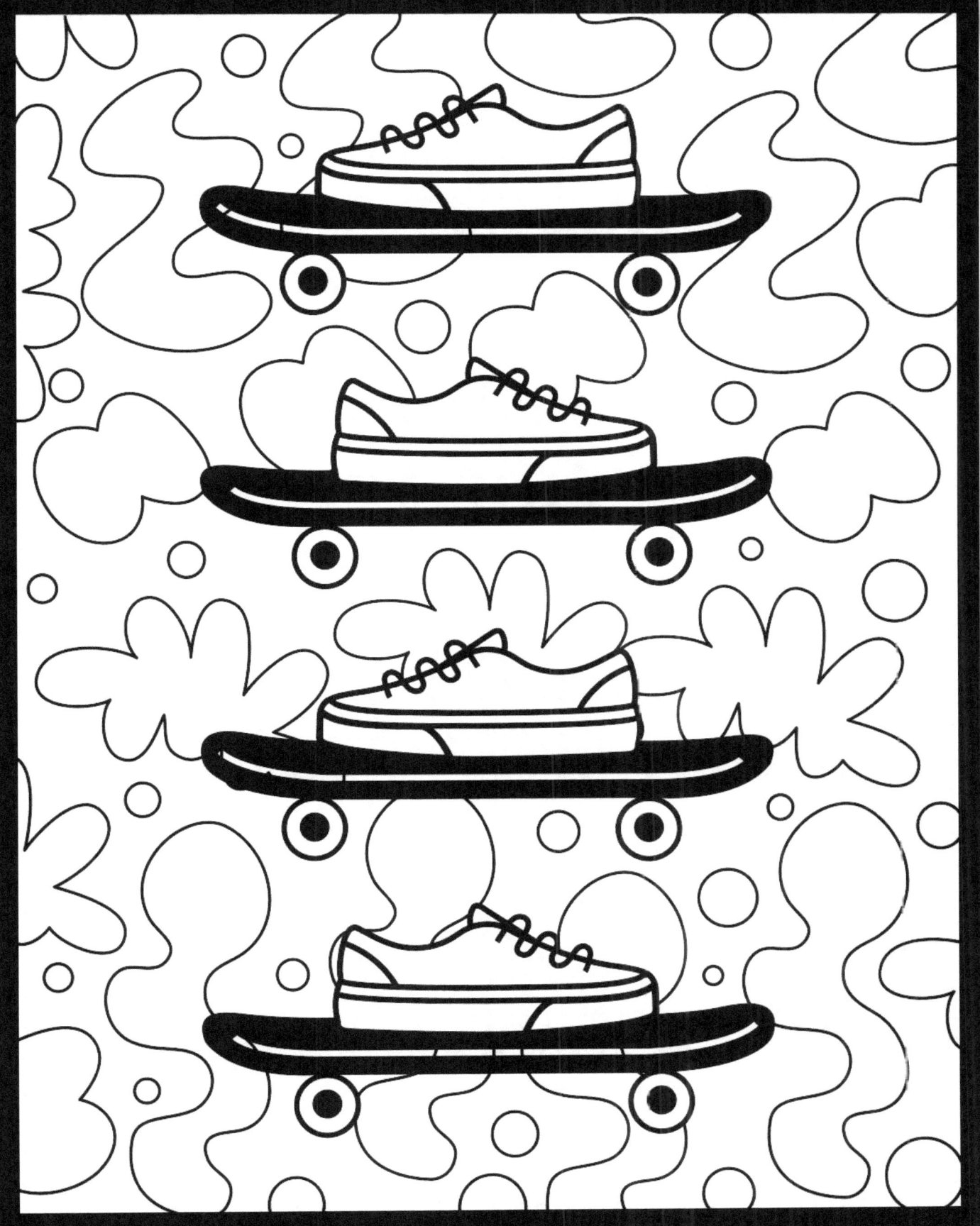

ROLLING WITH IT

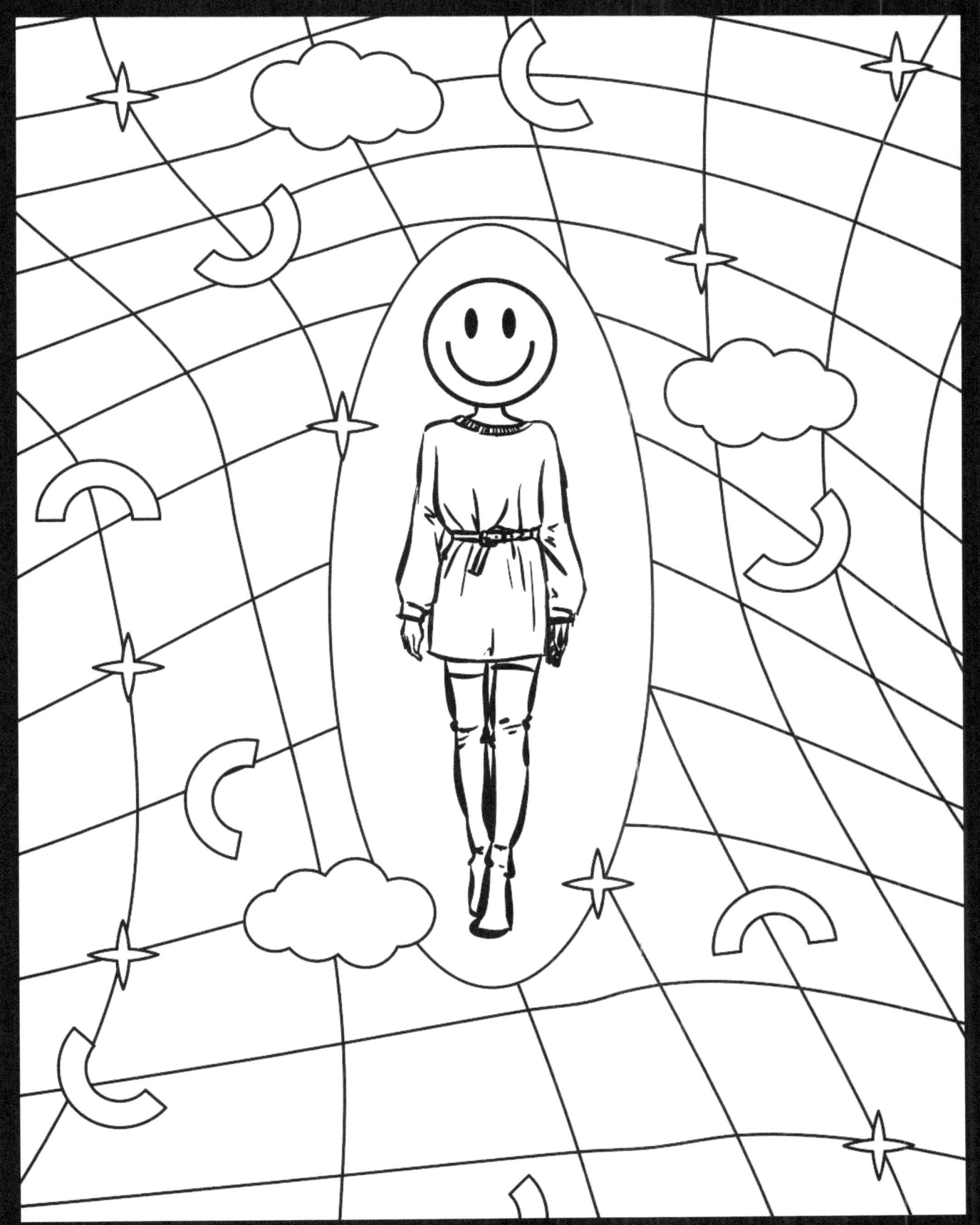

KEEP IT MOVING

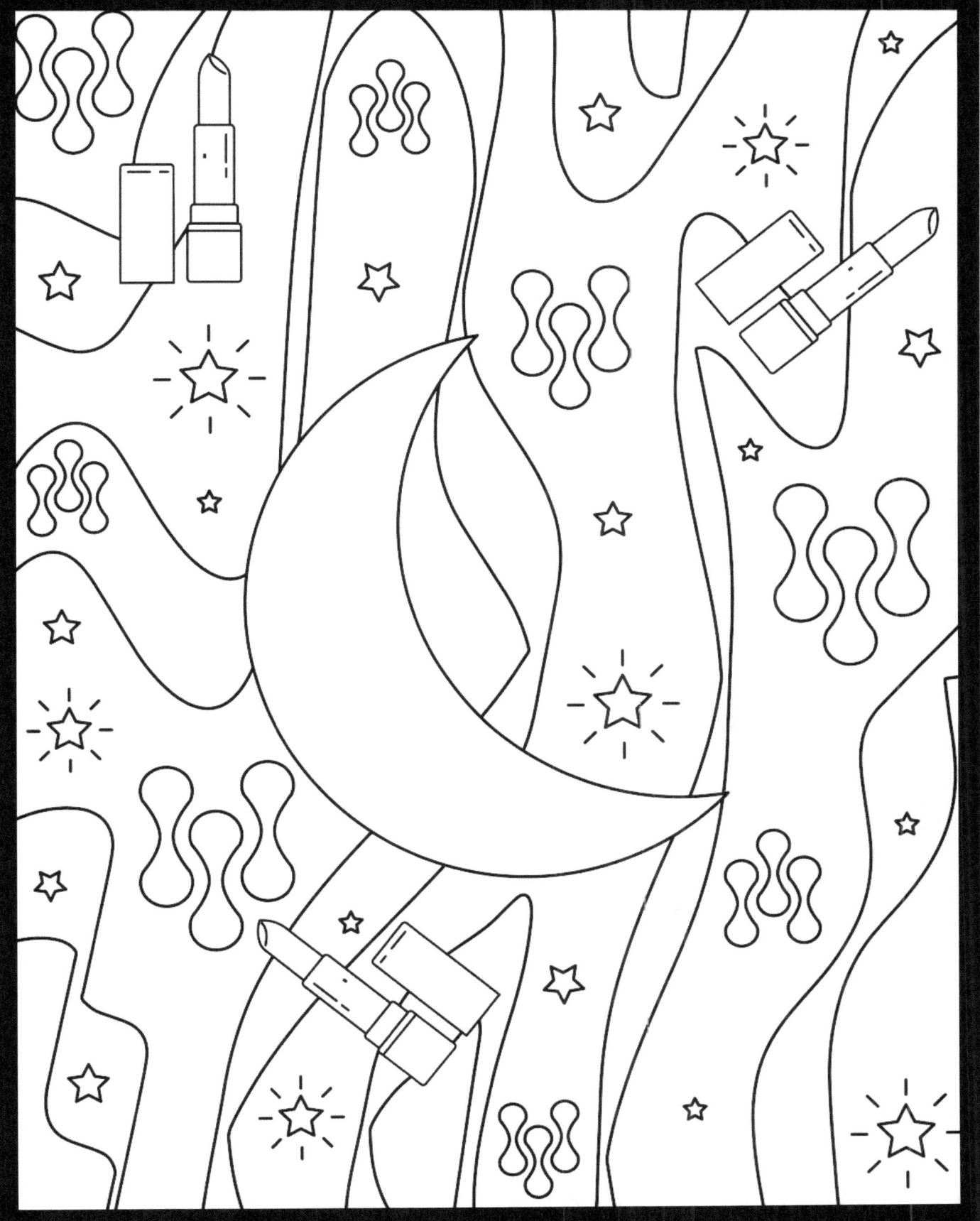

MOON MAGIC

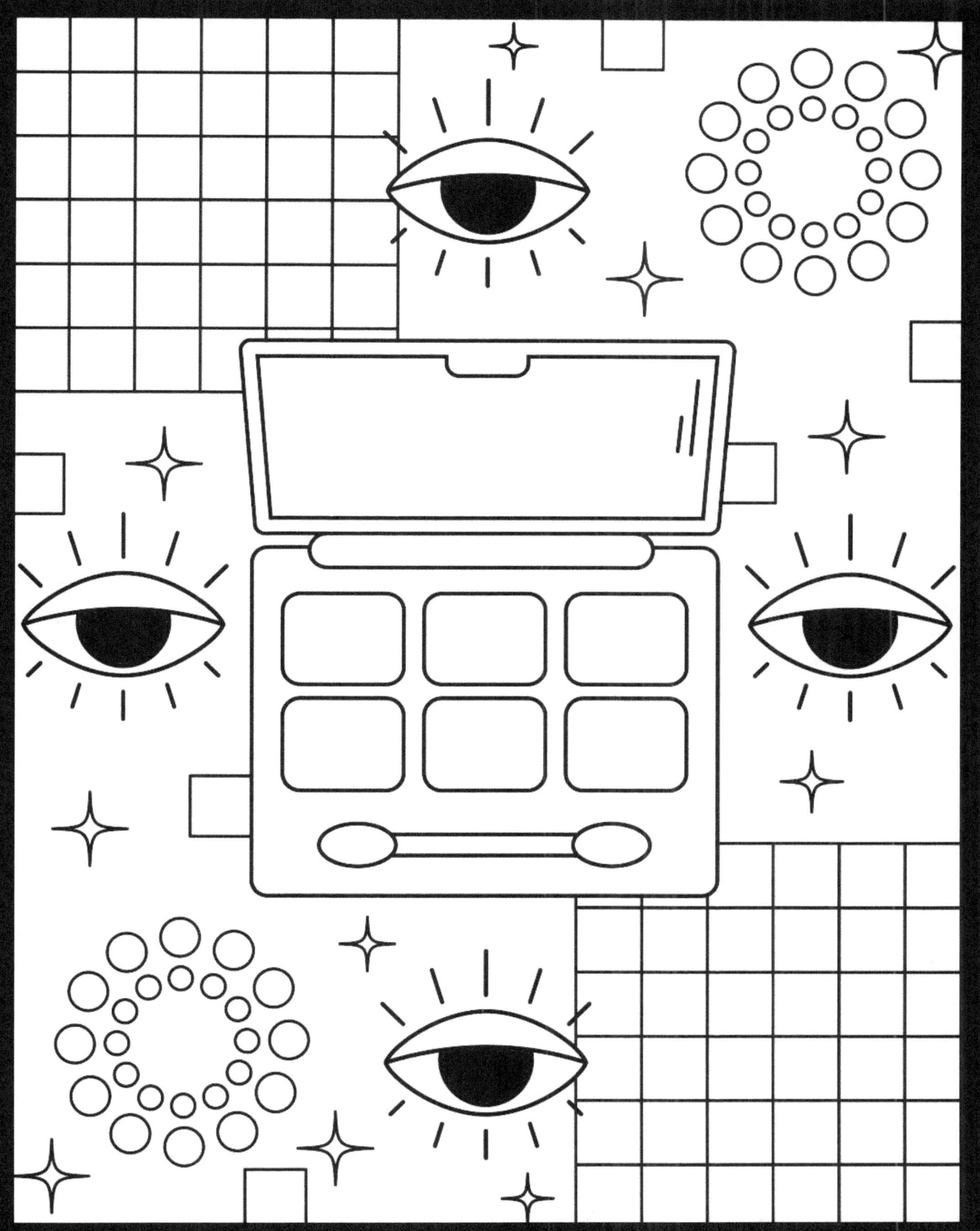

EYES AHEAD

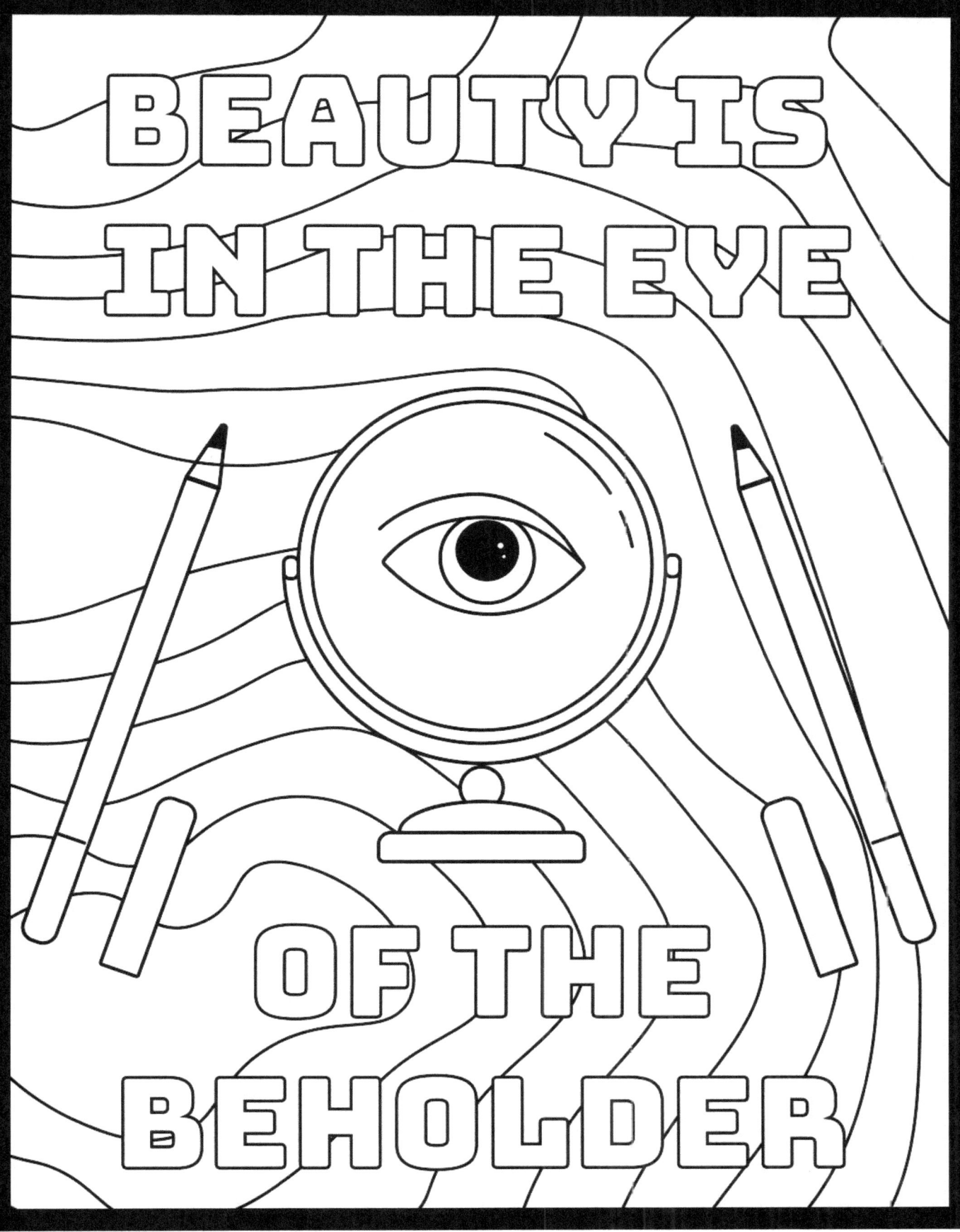

INSIDE AND OUTSIDE

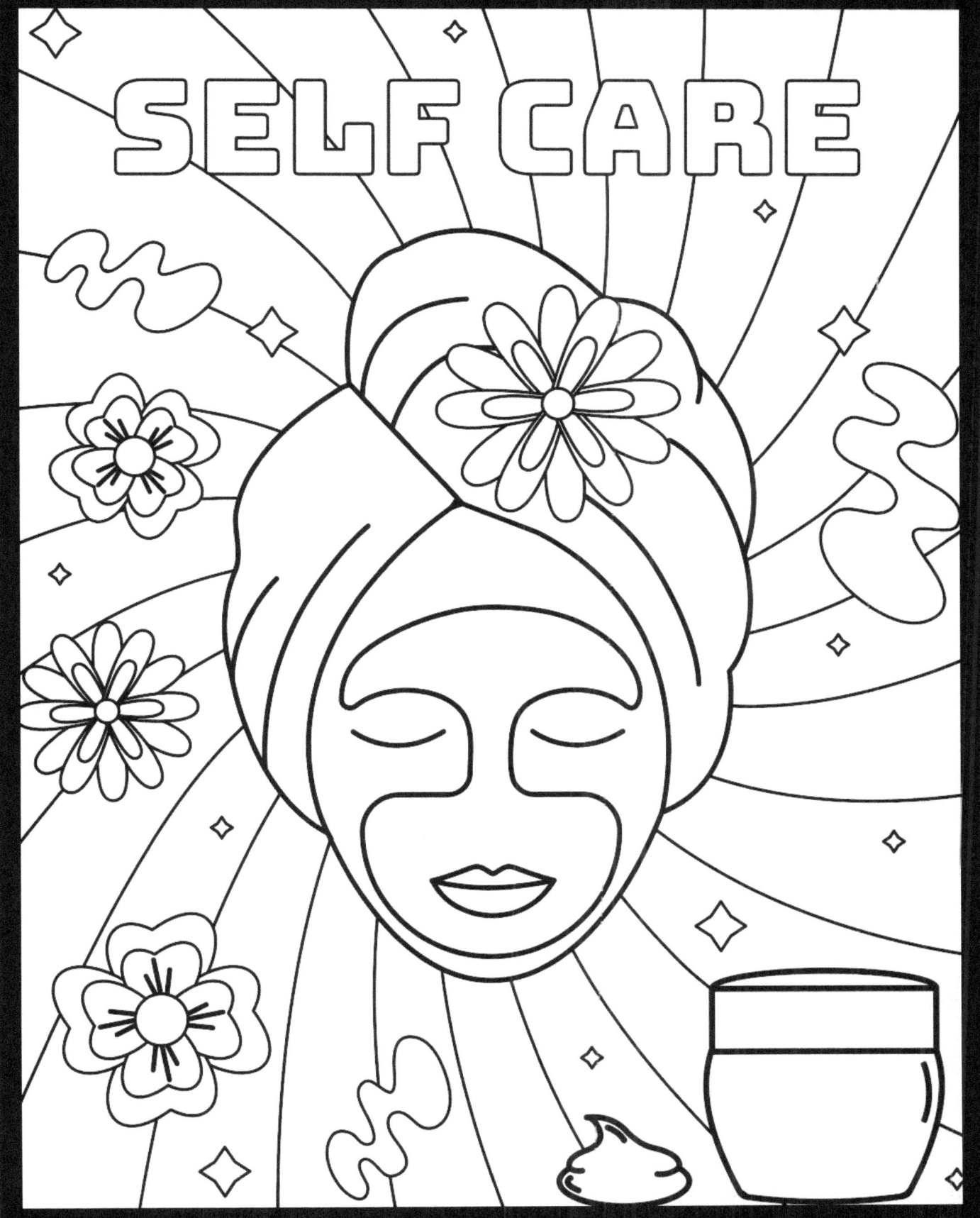

IMPORTANT

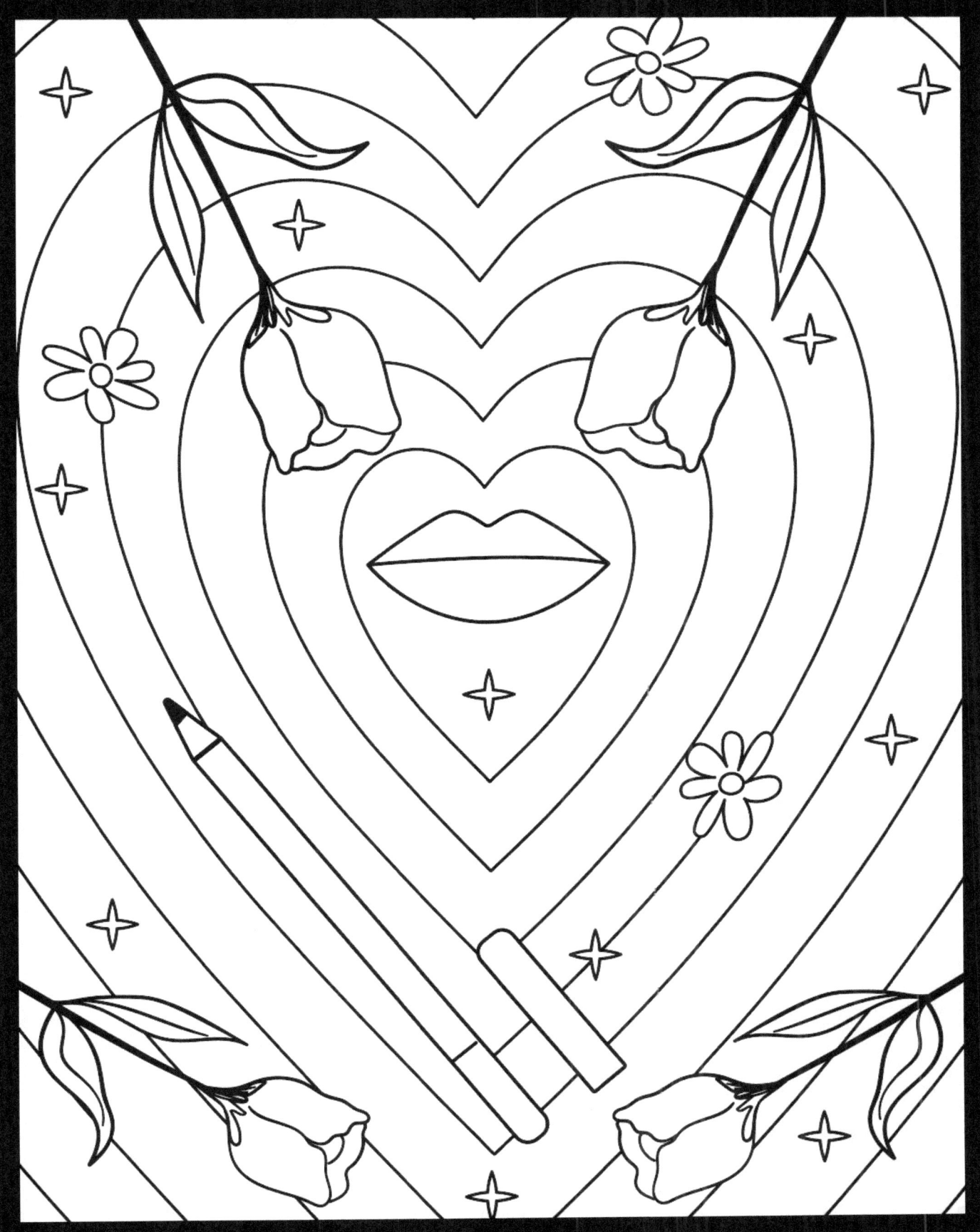

LUSCIOUS

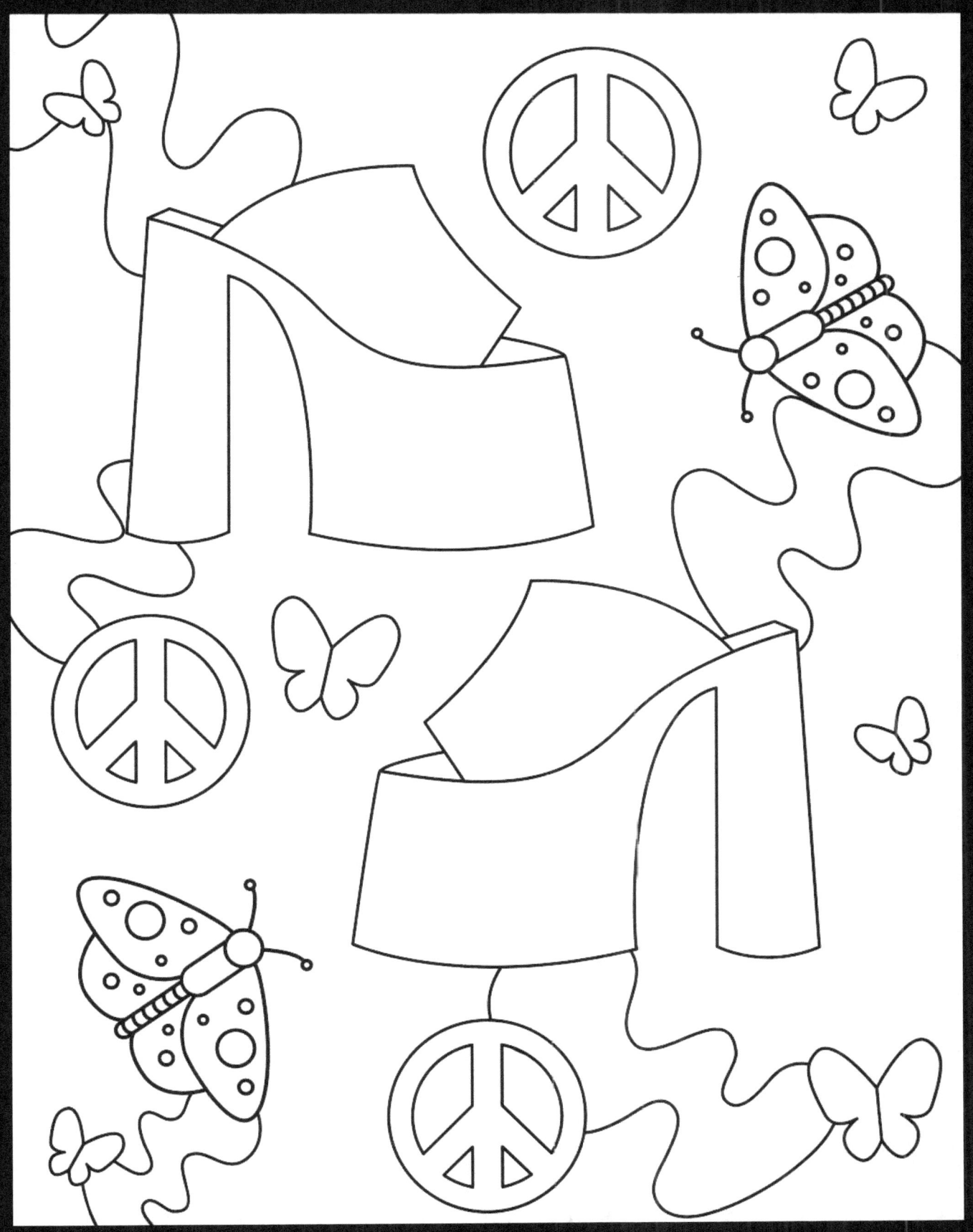

PLATFORMS AND PEACE

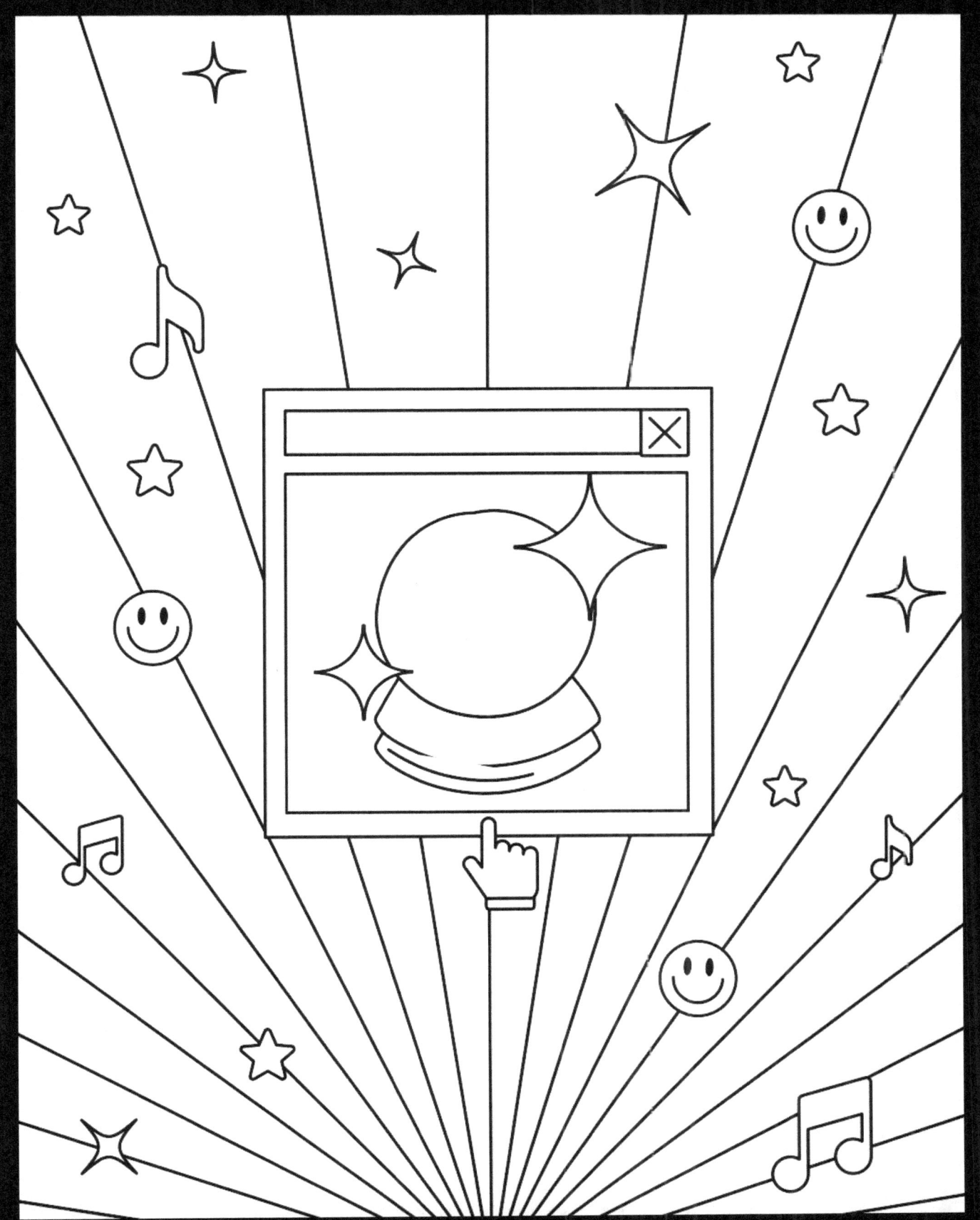

GOOD FORTUNE FUTURE

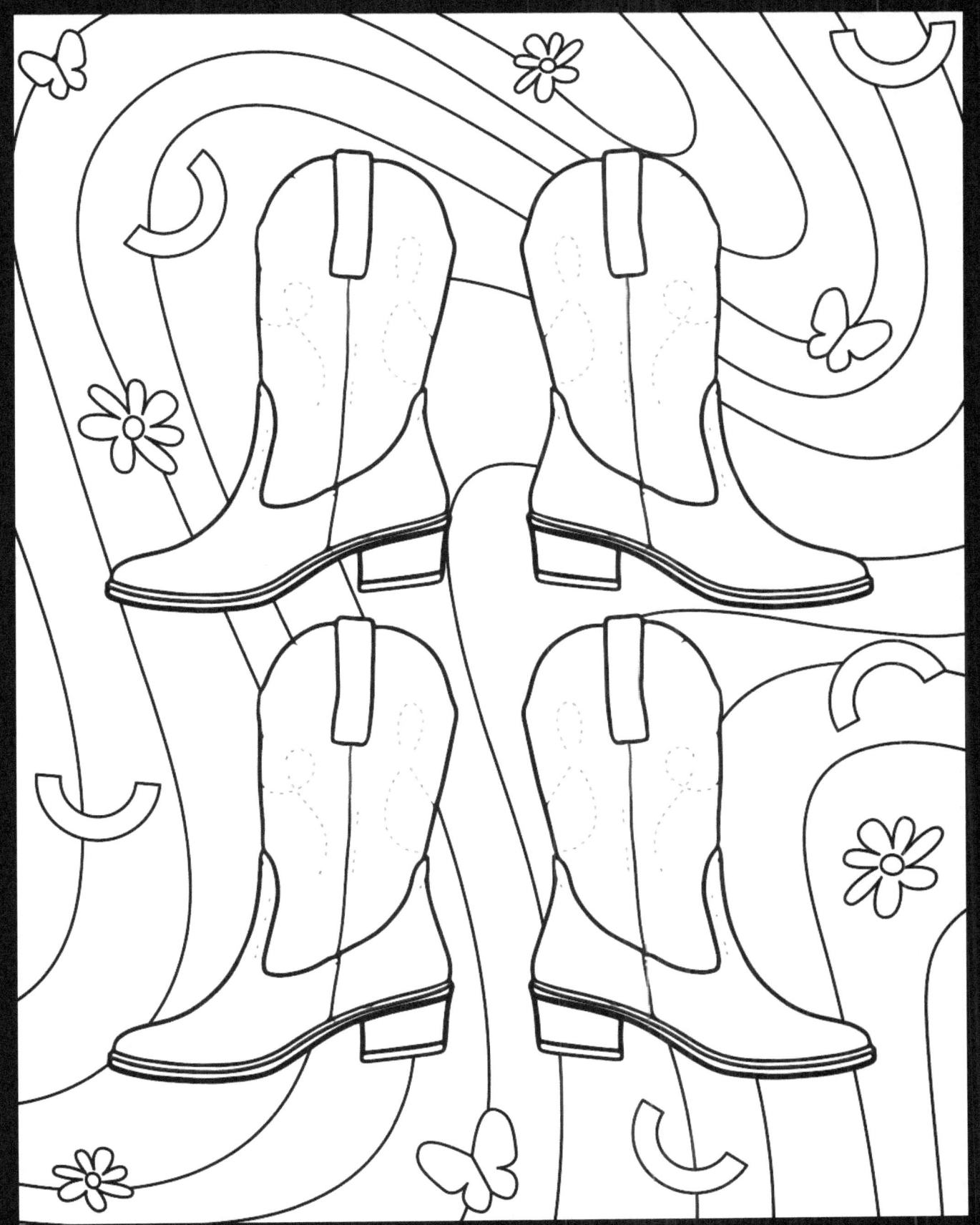

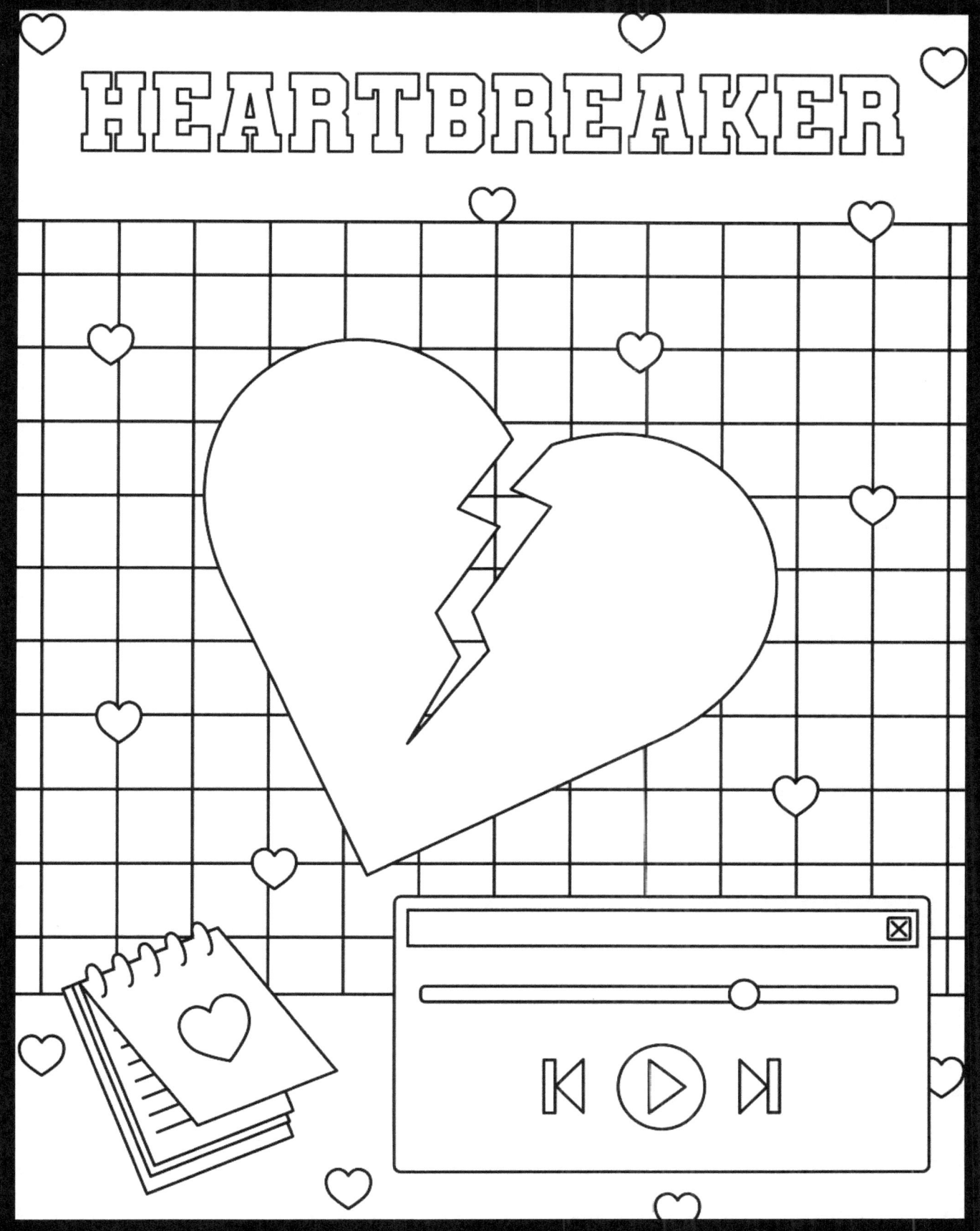

HEART BREAKER

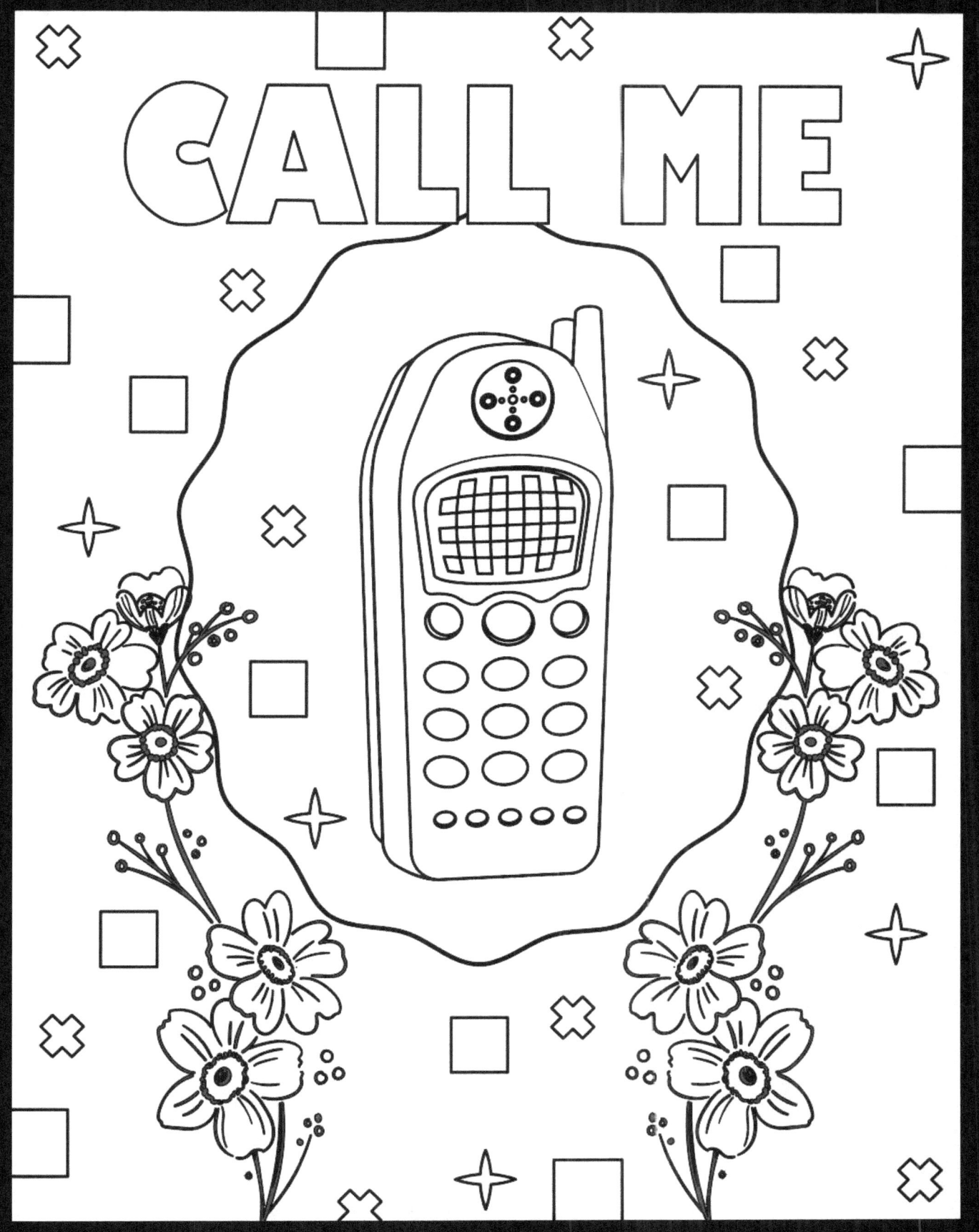

CALL ME

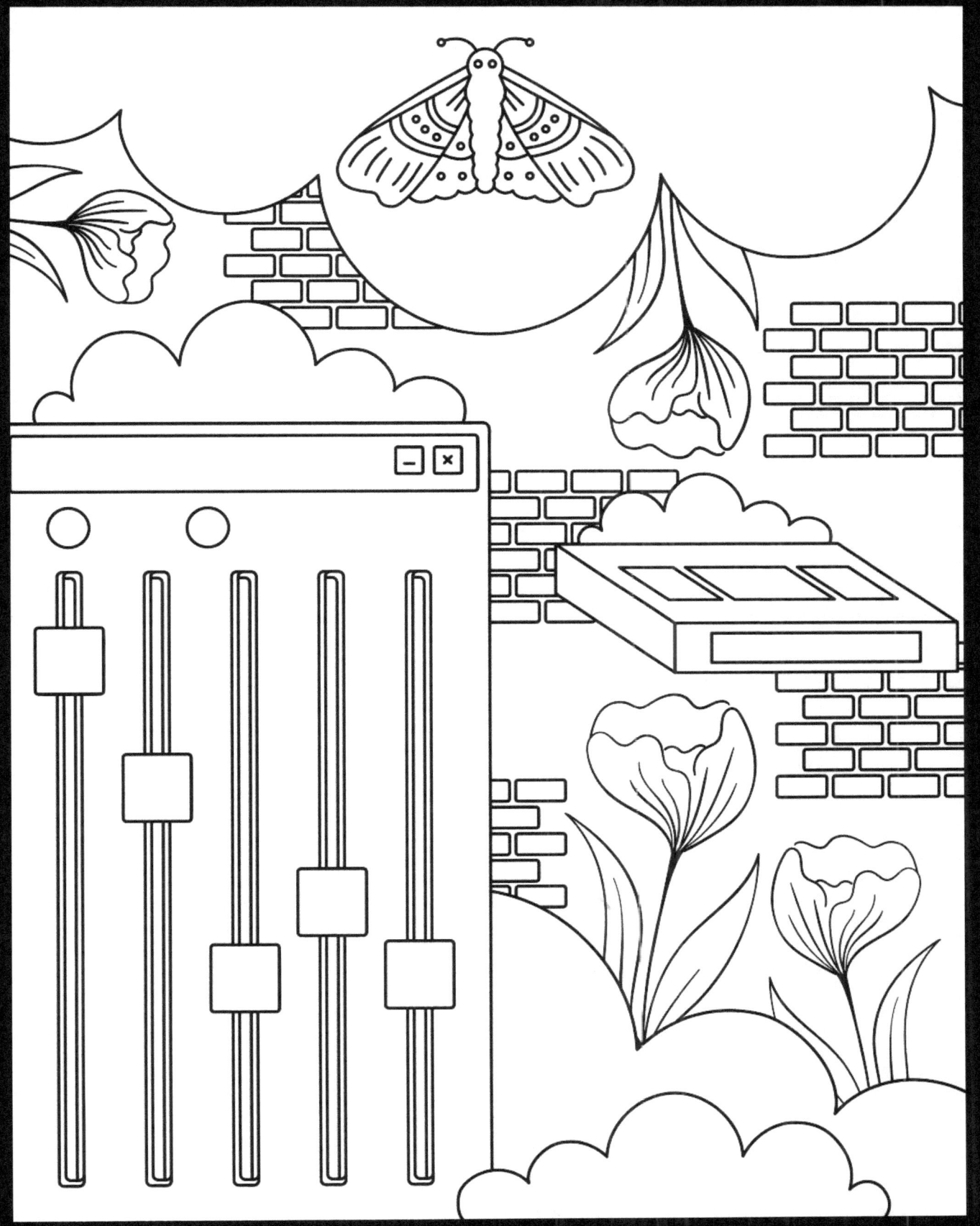

TUNING IN

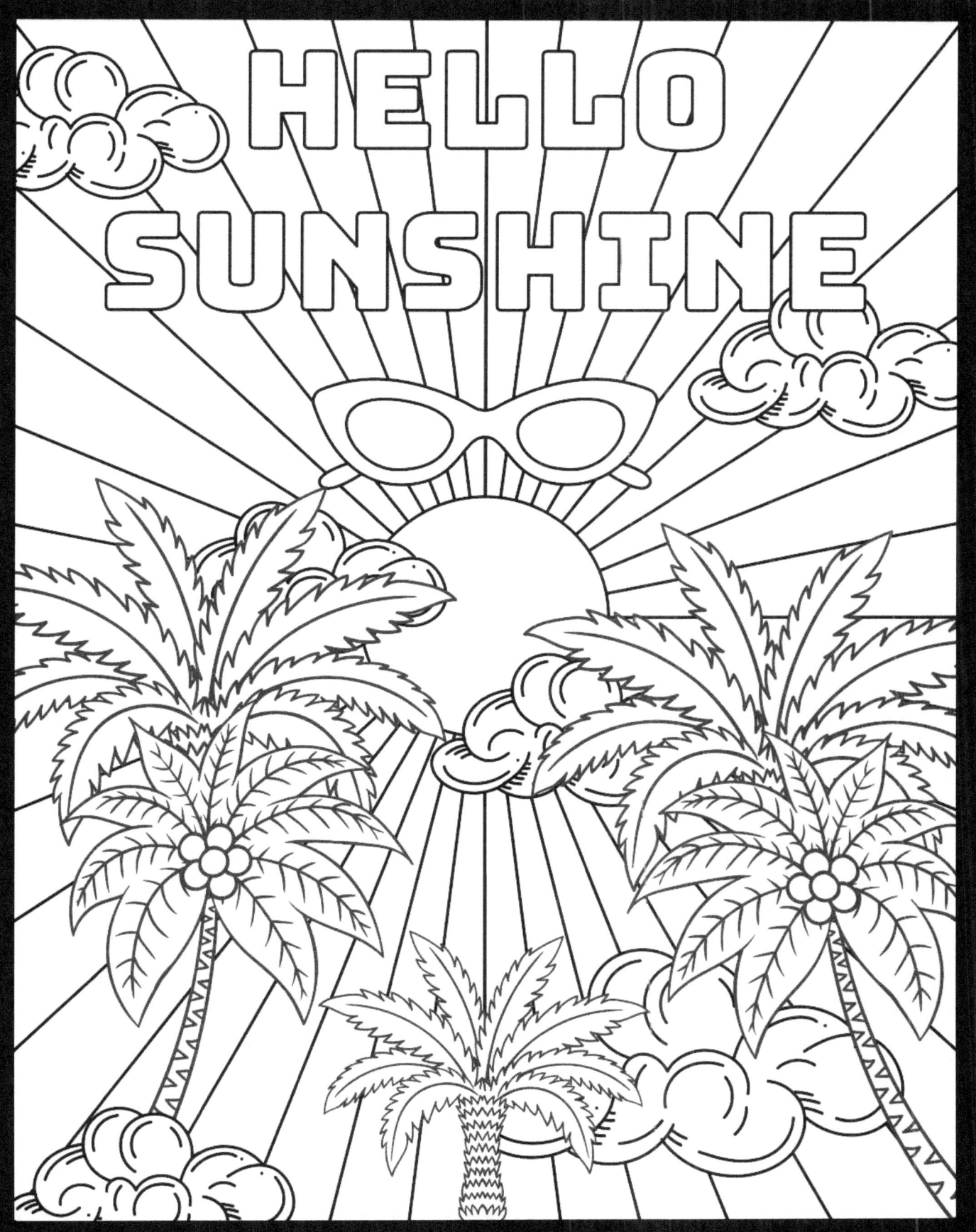

POSITIVE SKIES

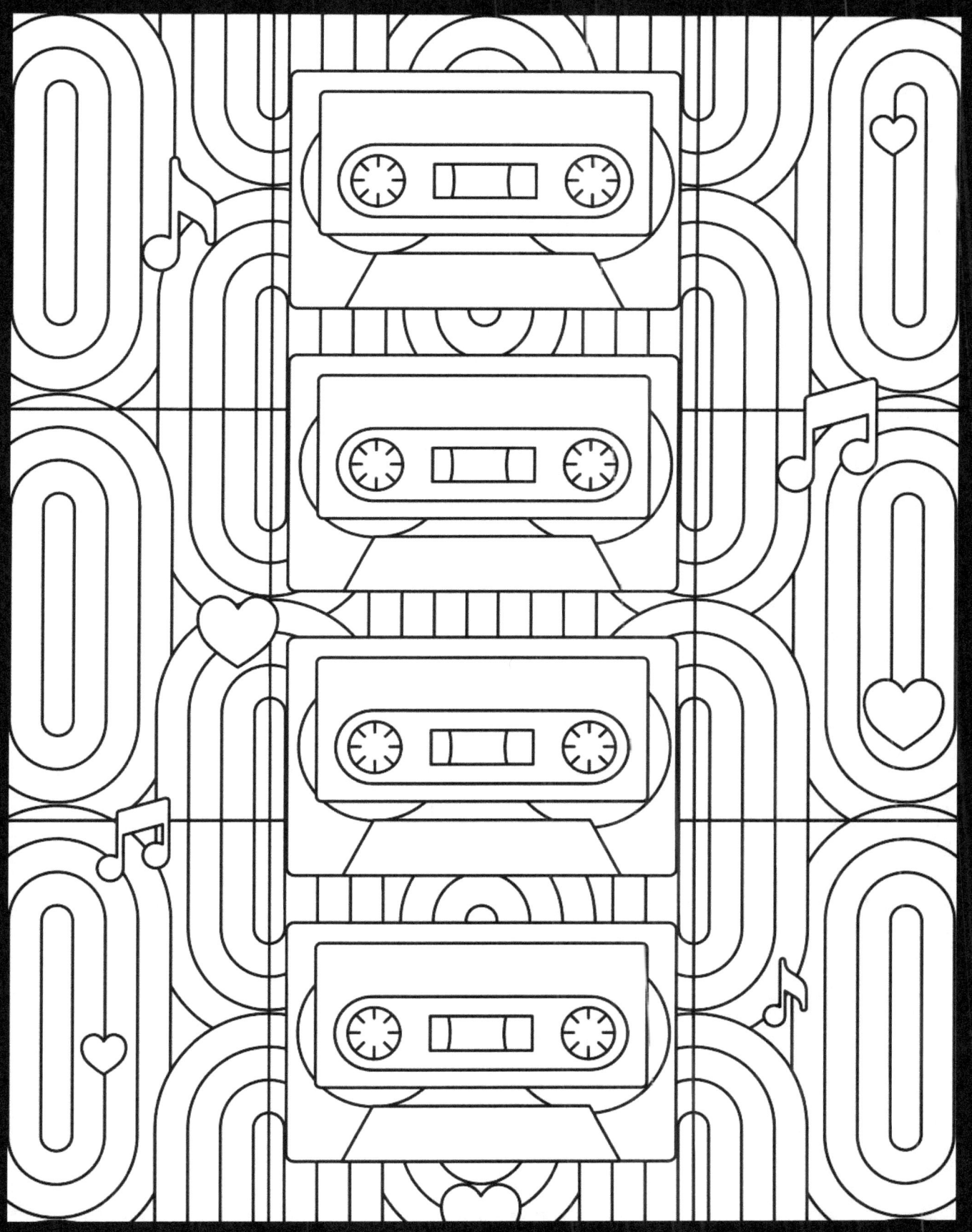

REMIX

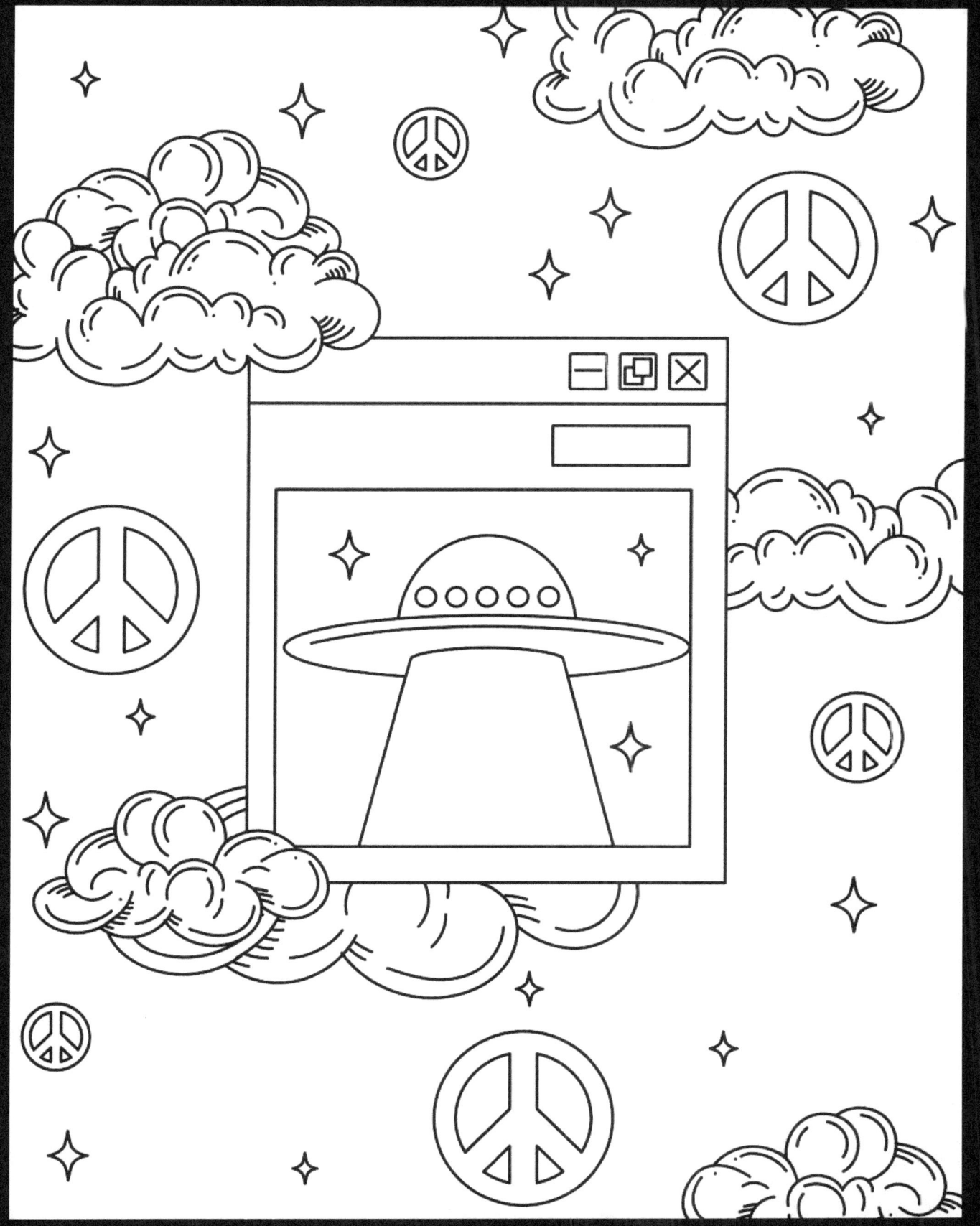

WE COME IN PEACE

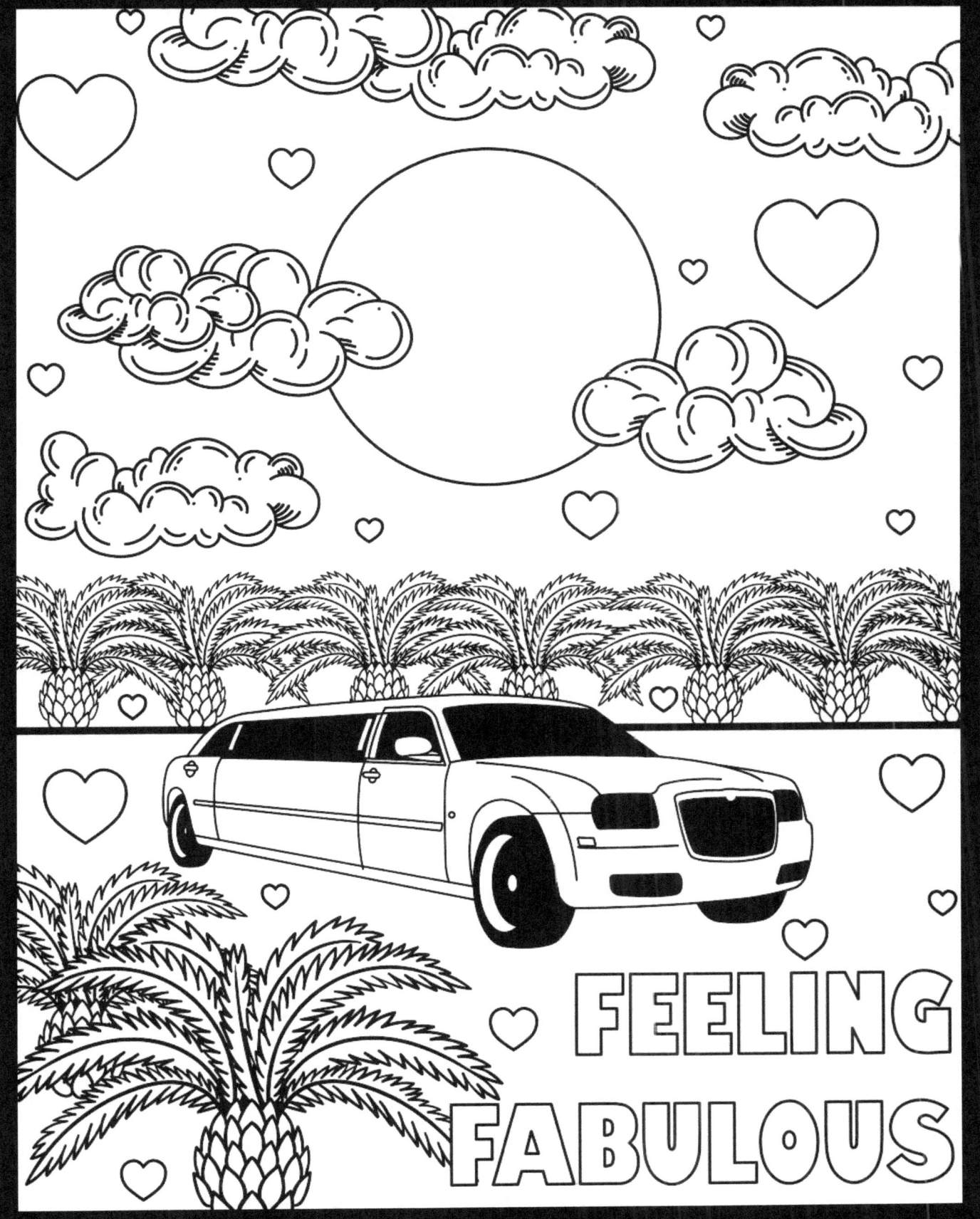

GET ME OUT OF HERE

RADIANT

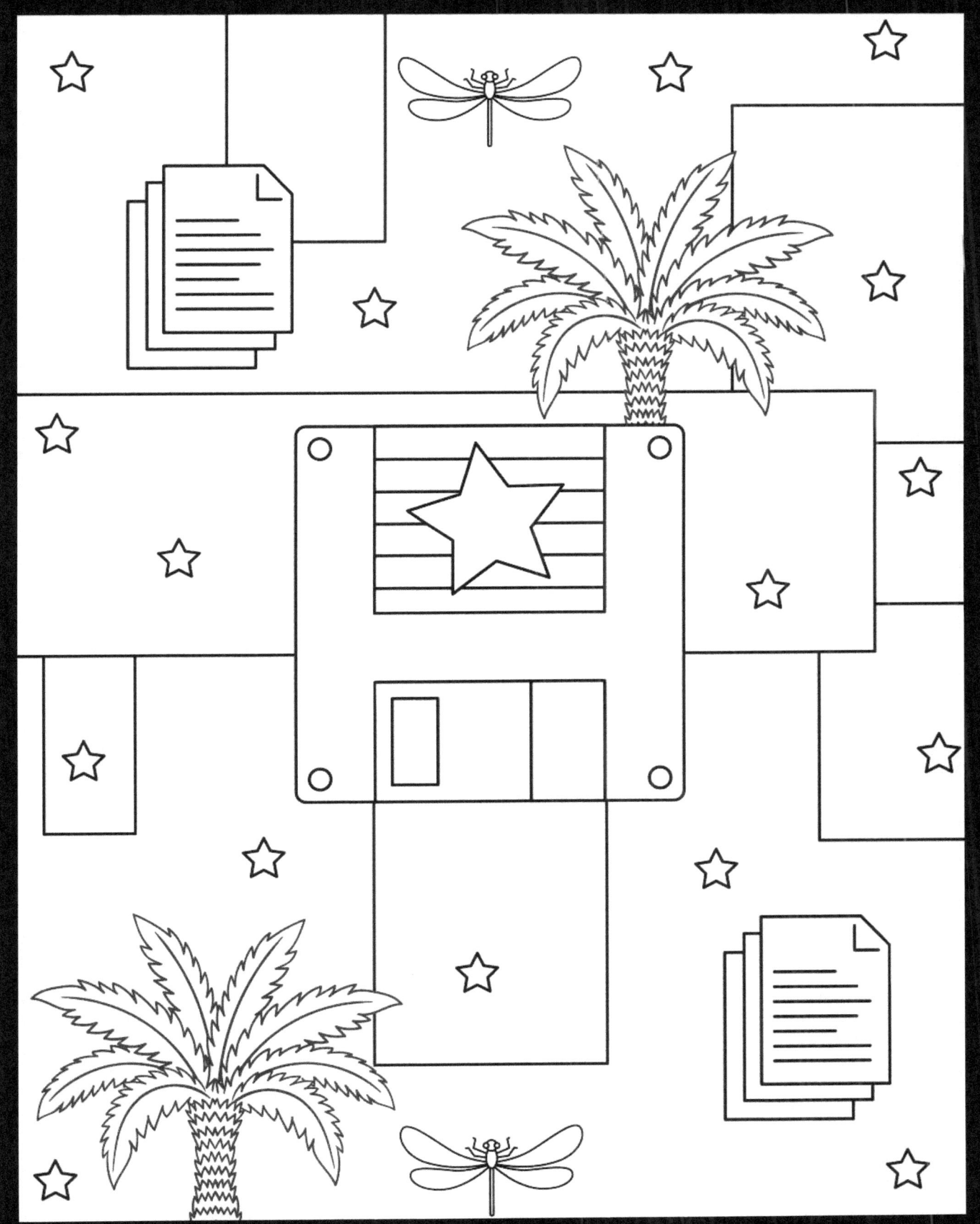

SAVED

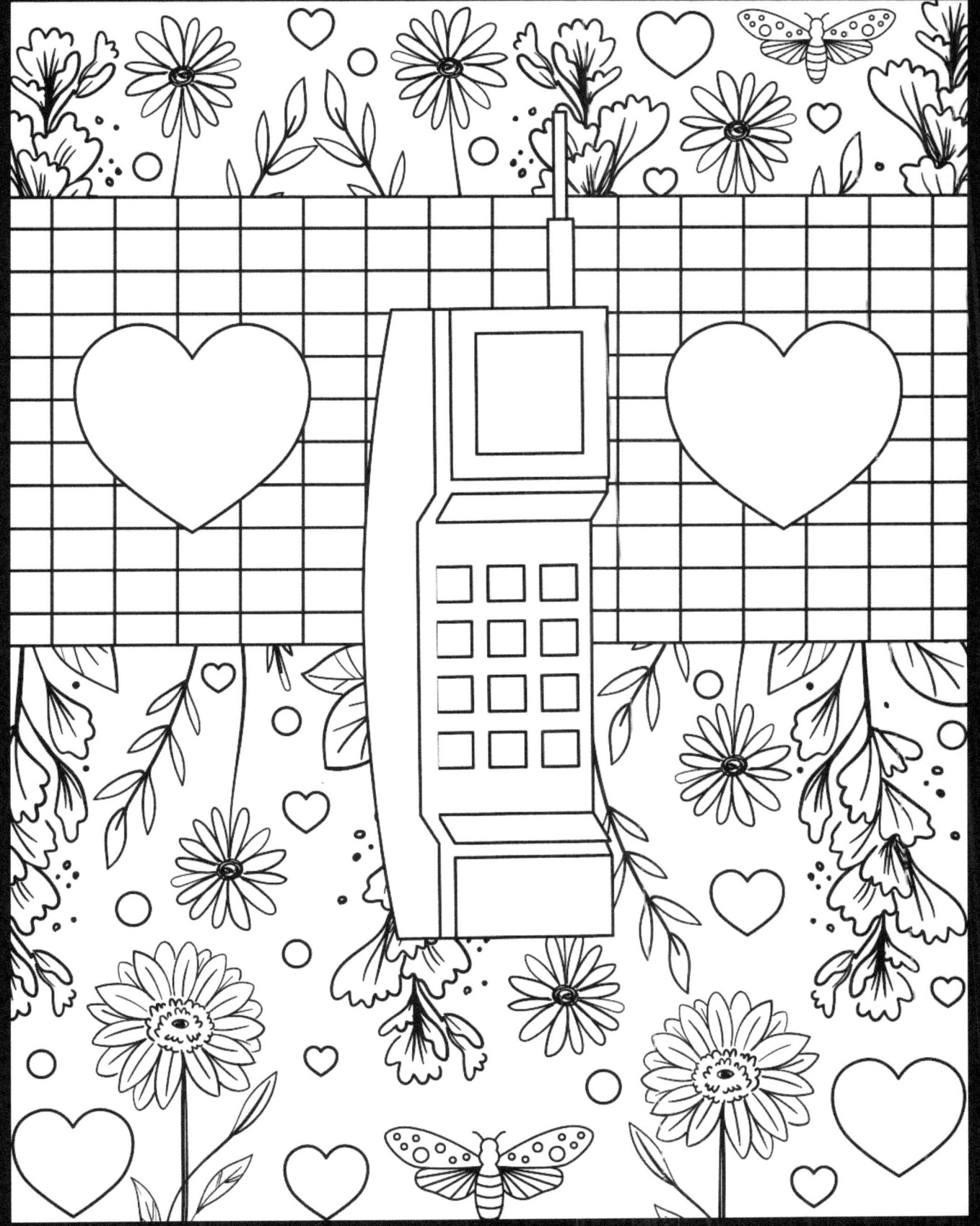

CLASSIC

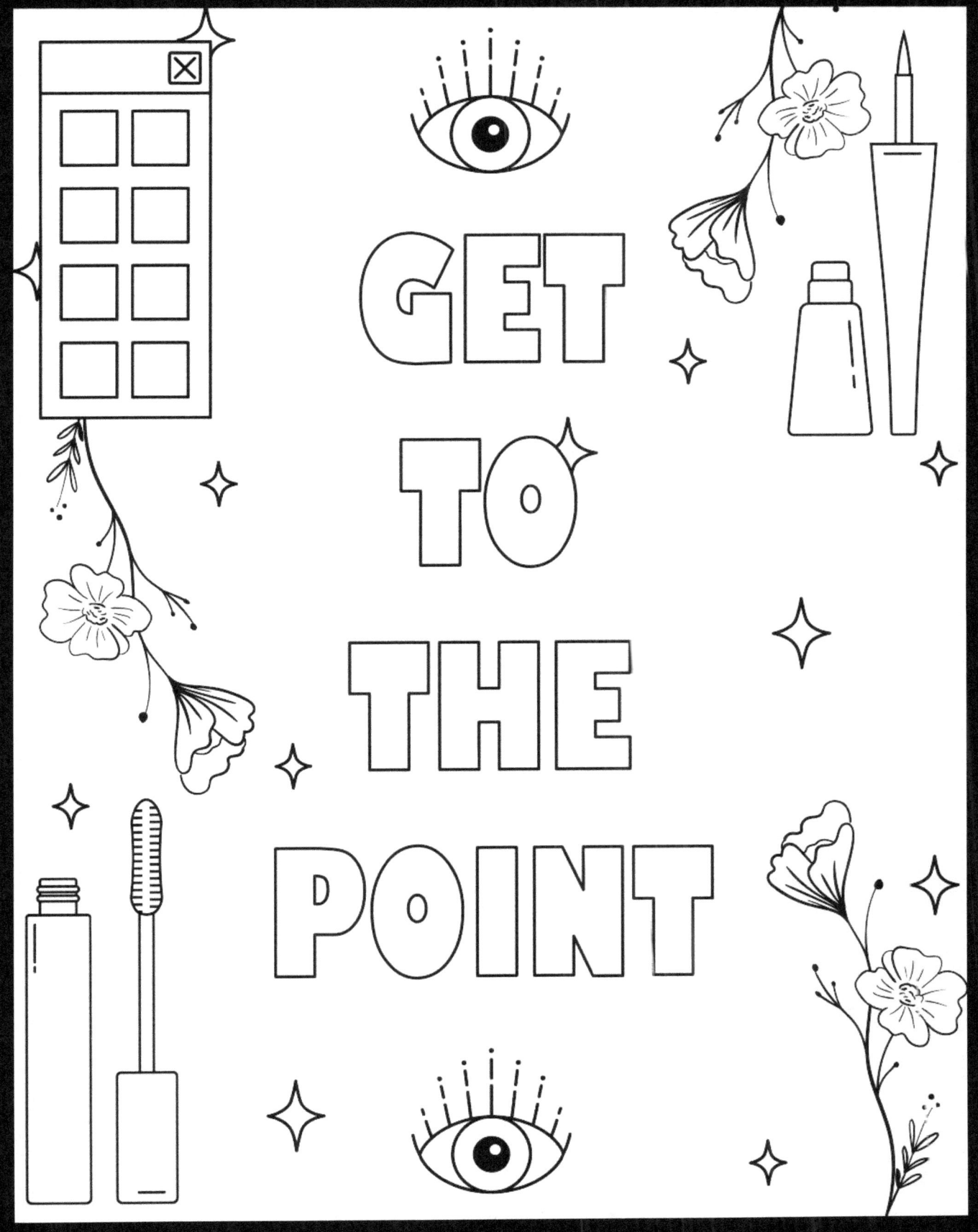

MAKE IT SHARP

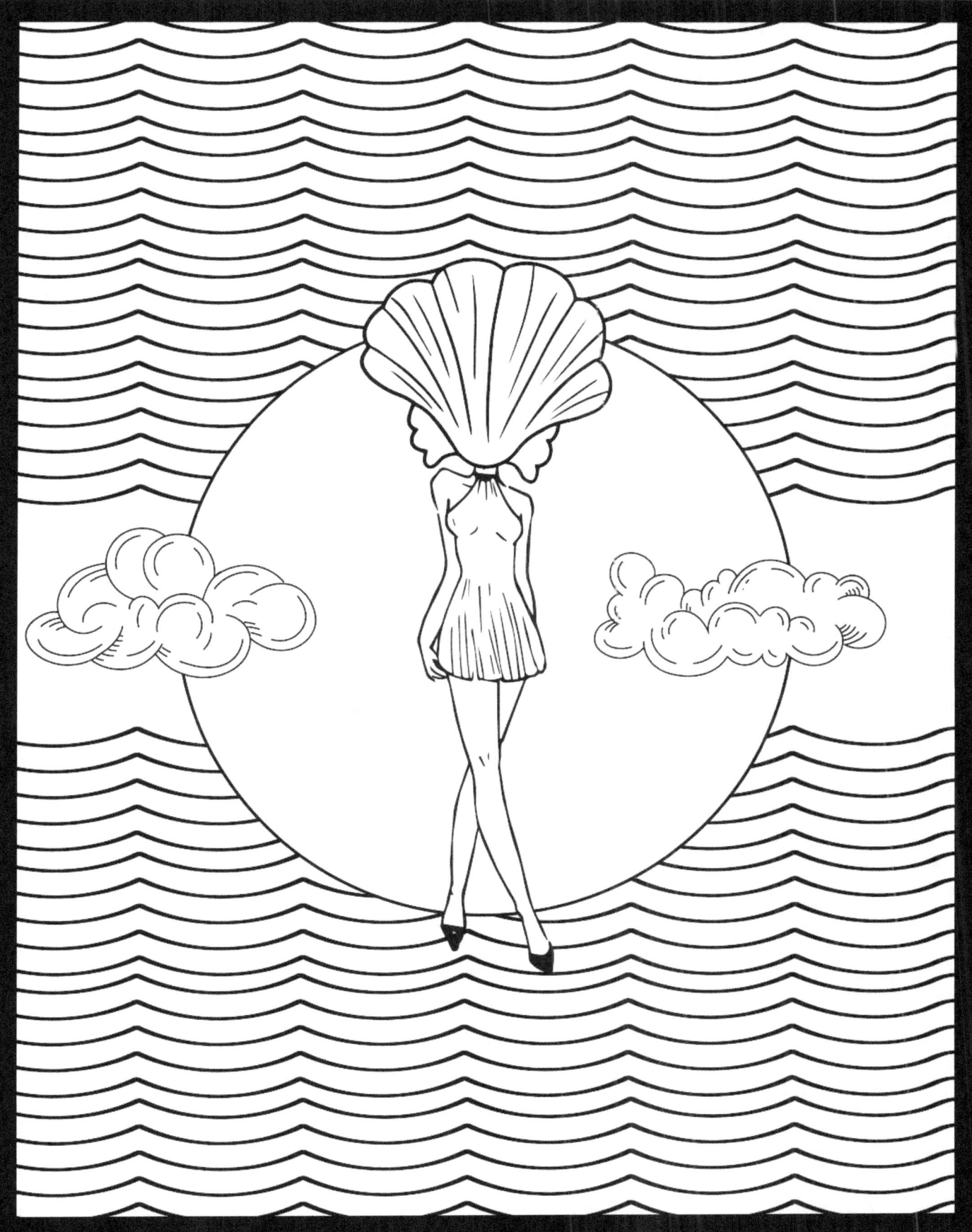

SHELL YEAH

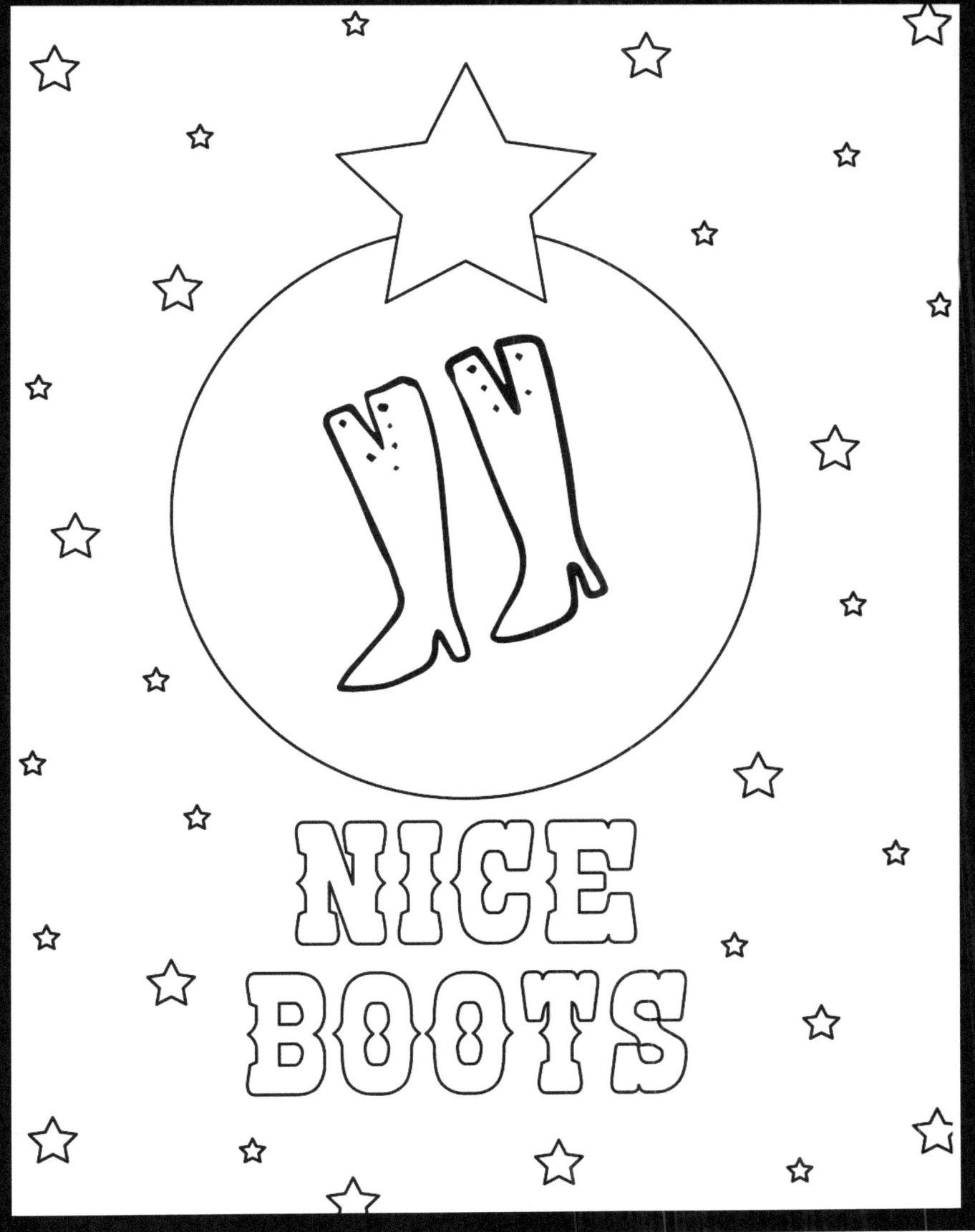

FOR WALKING

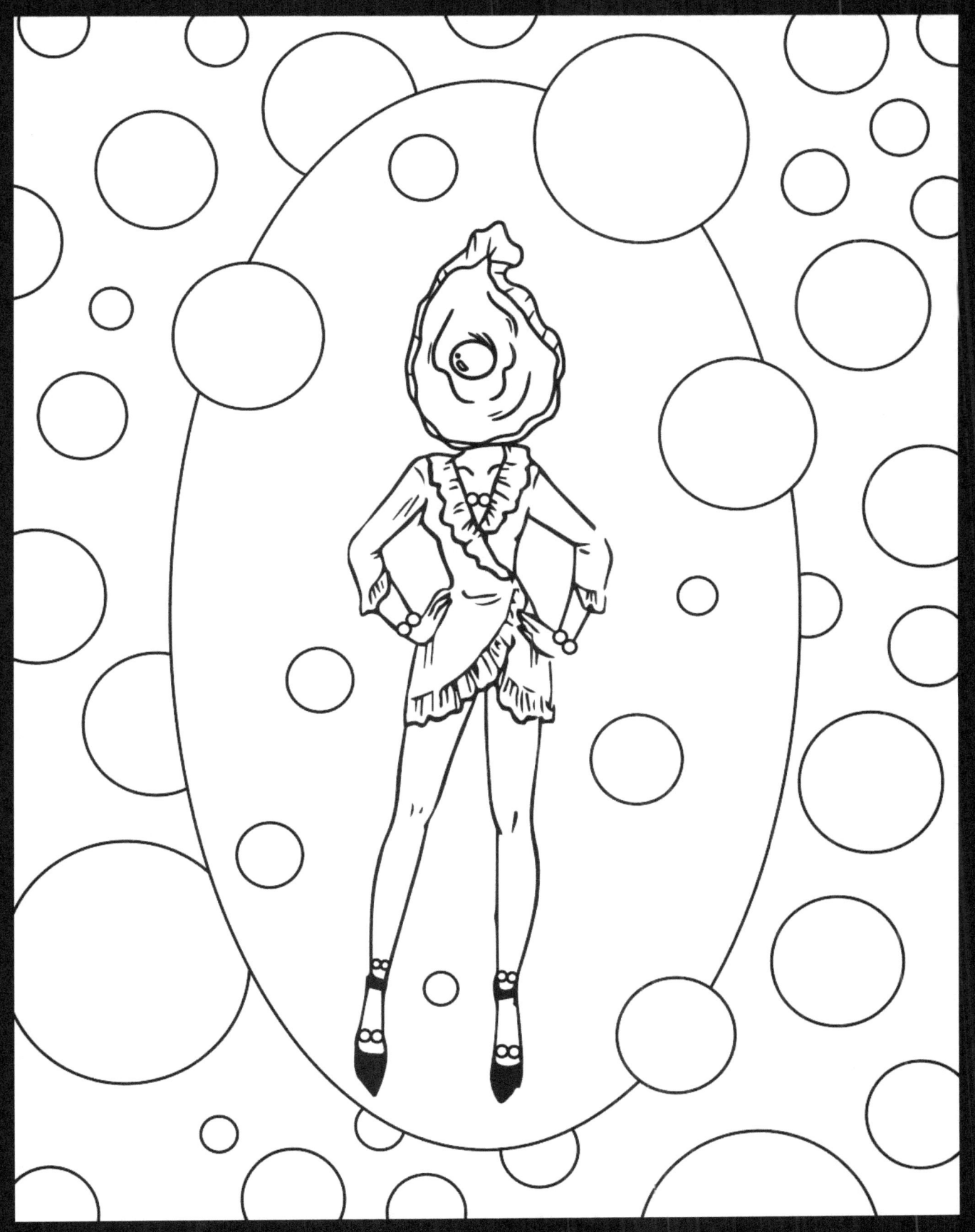

PEARL GIRL.

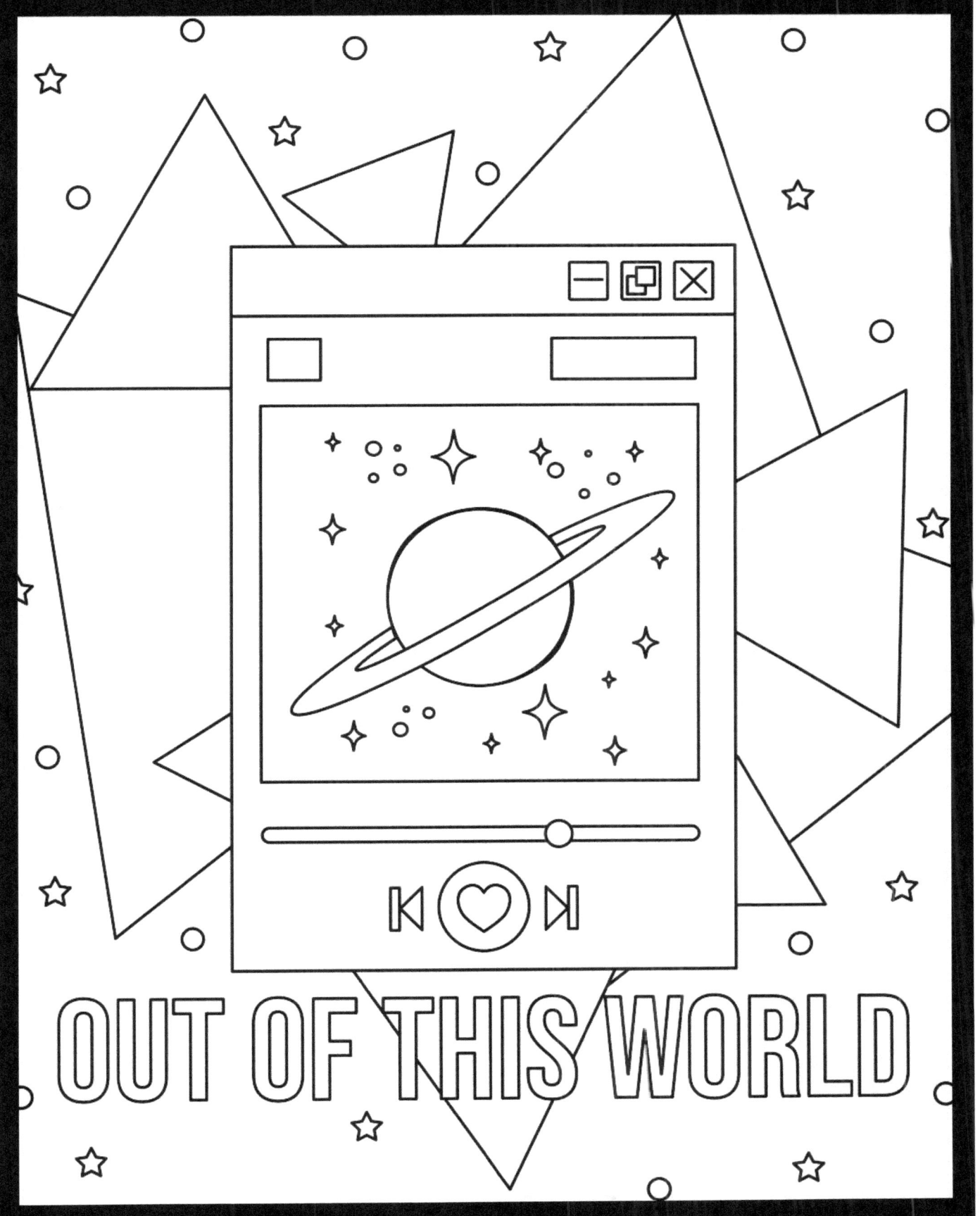

FREQUENCY

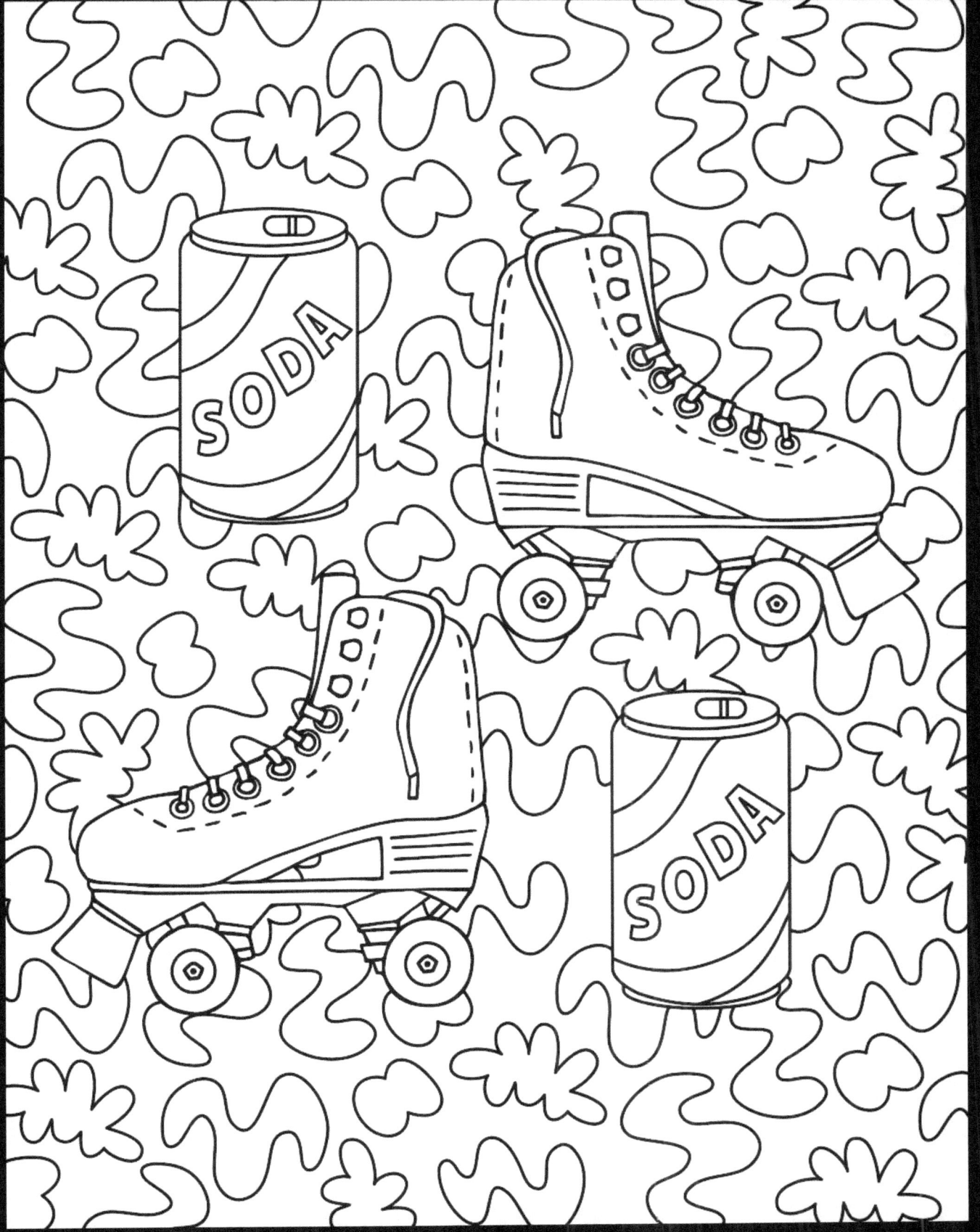

SODAS AND SKATES

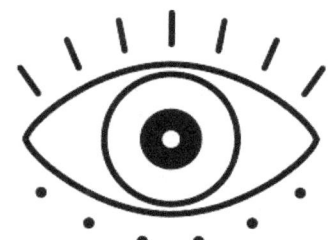
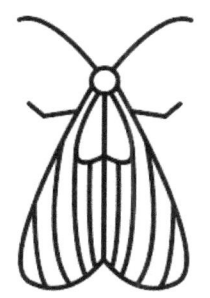
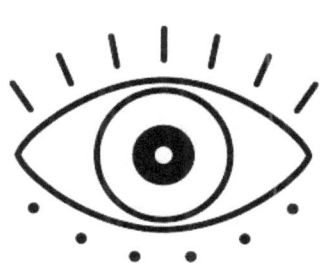
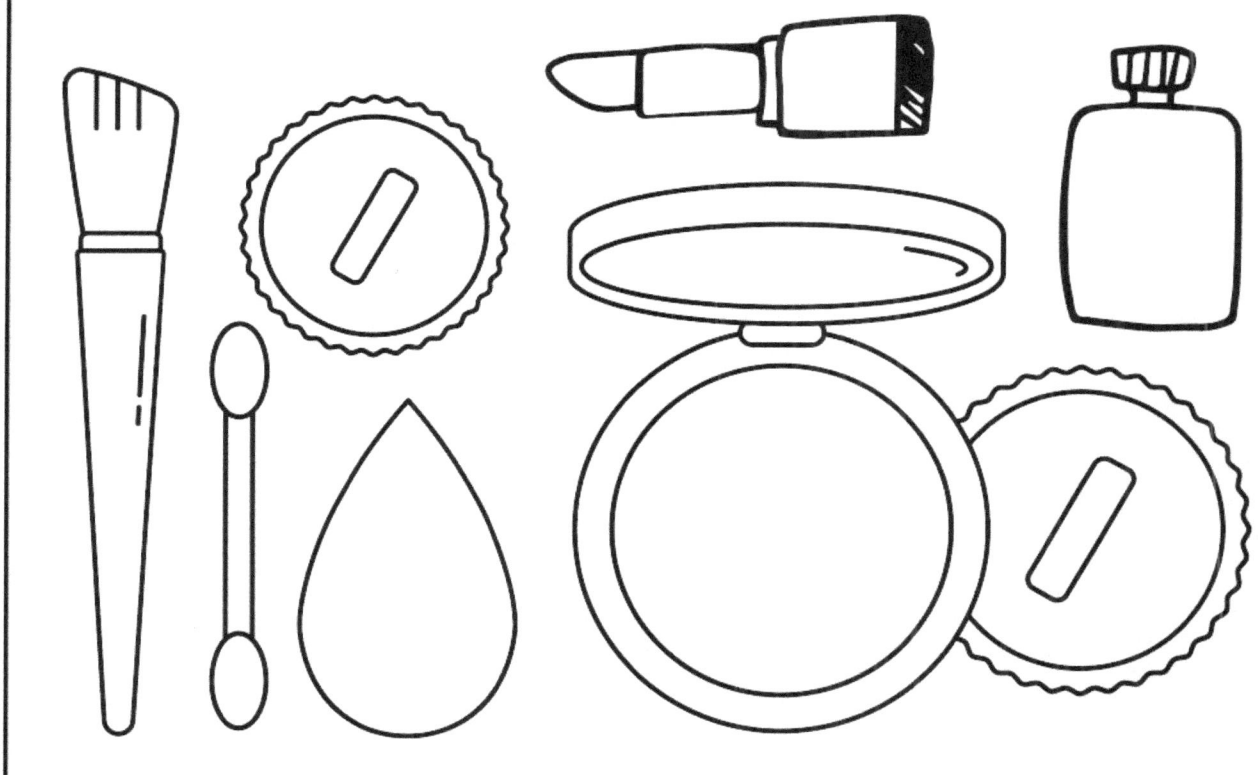
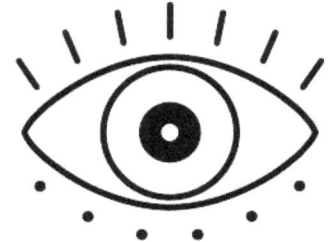
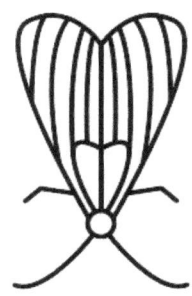
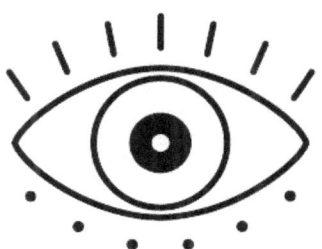

MAKING IT UP

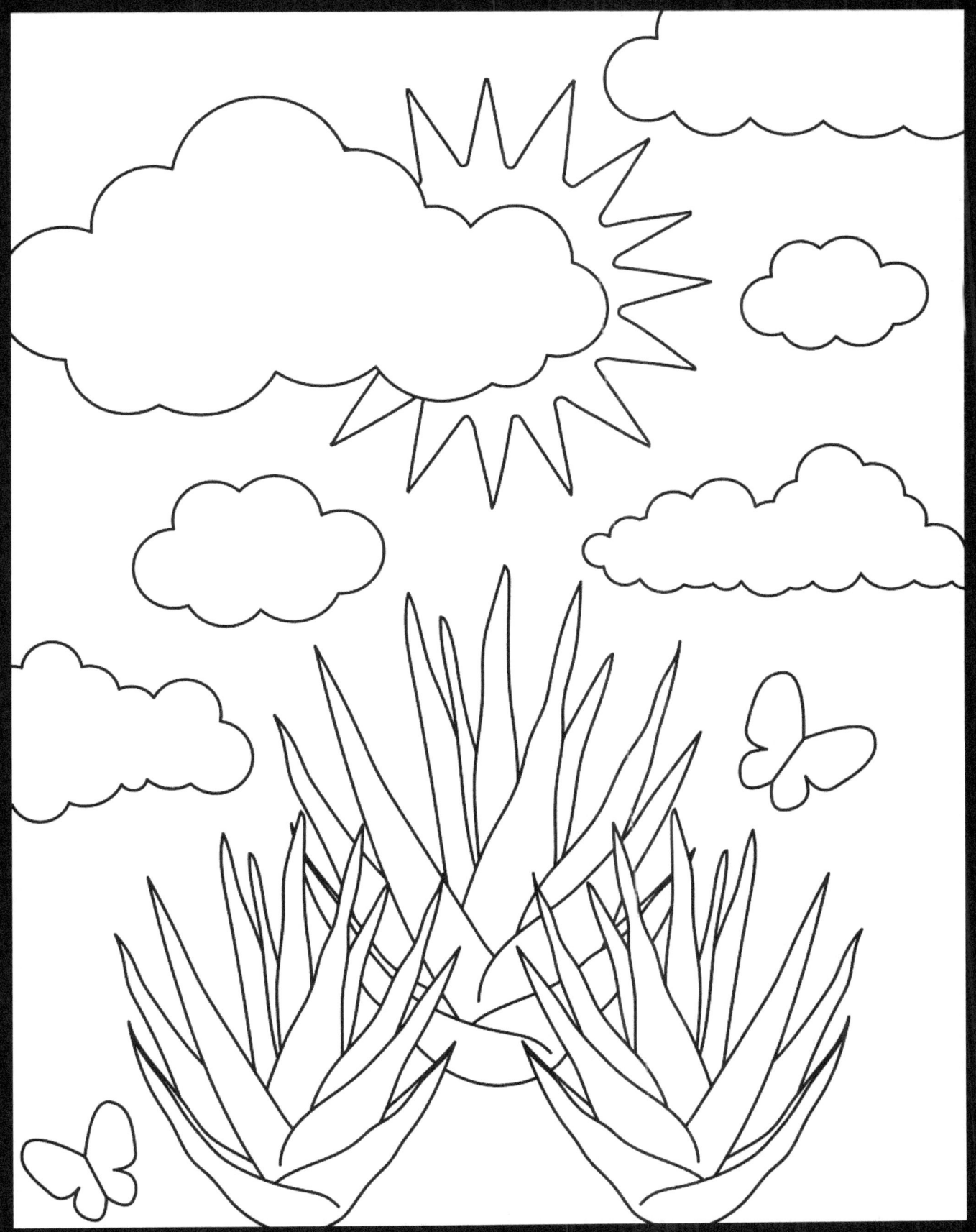

SERENE THINGS

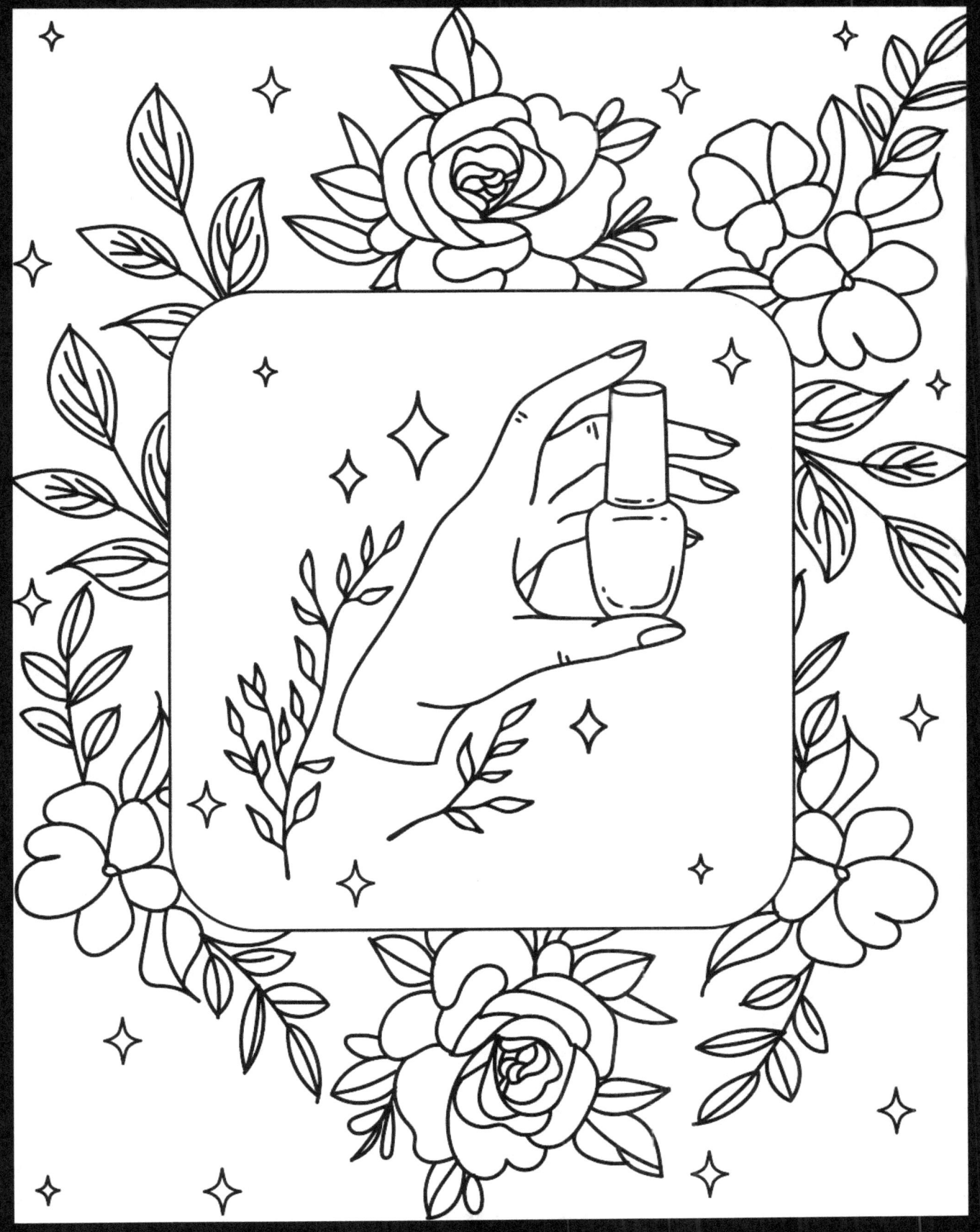

TOUCH UP

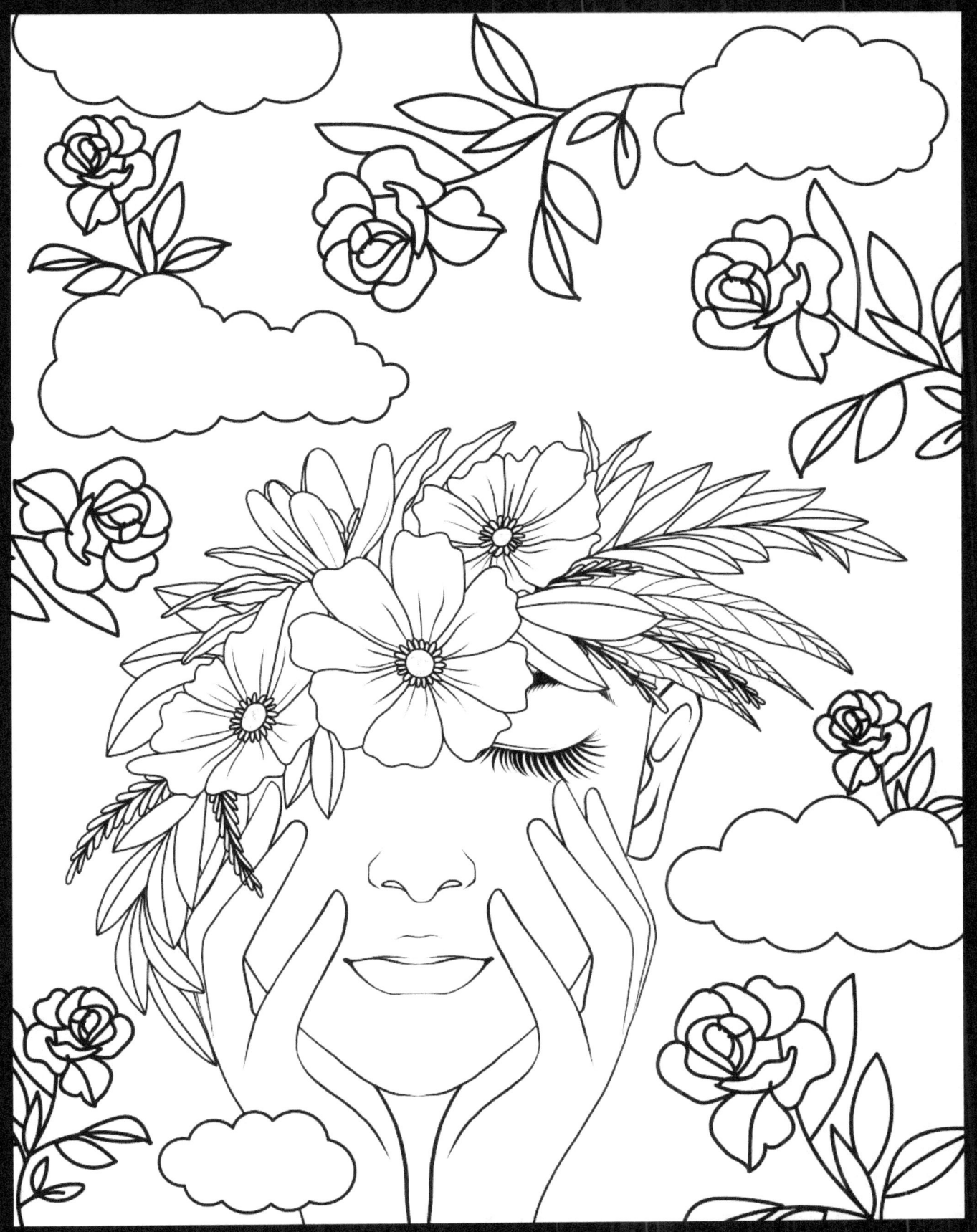

DAYDREAMS

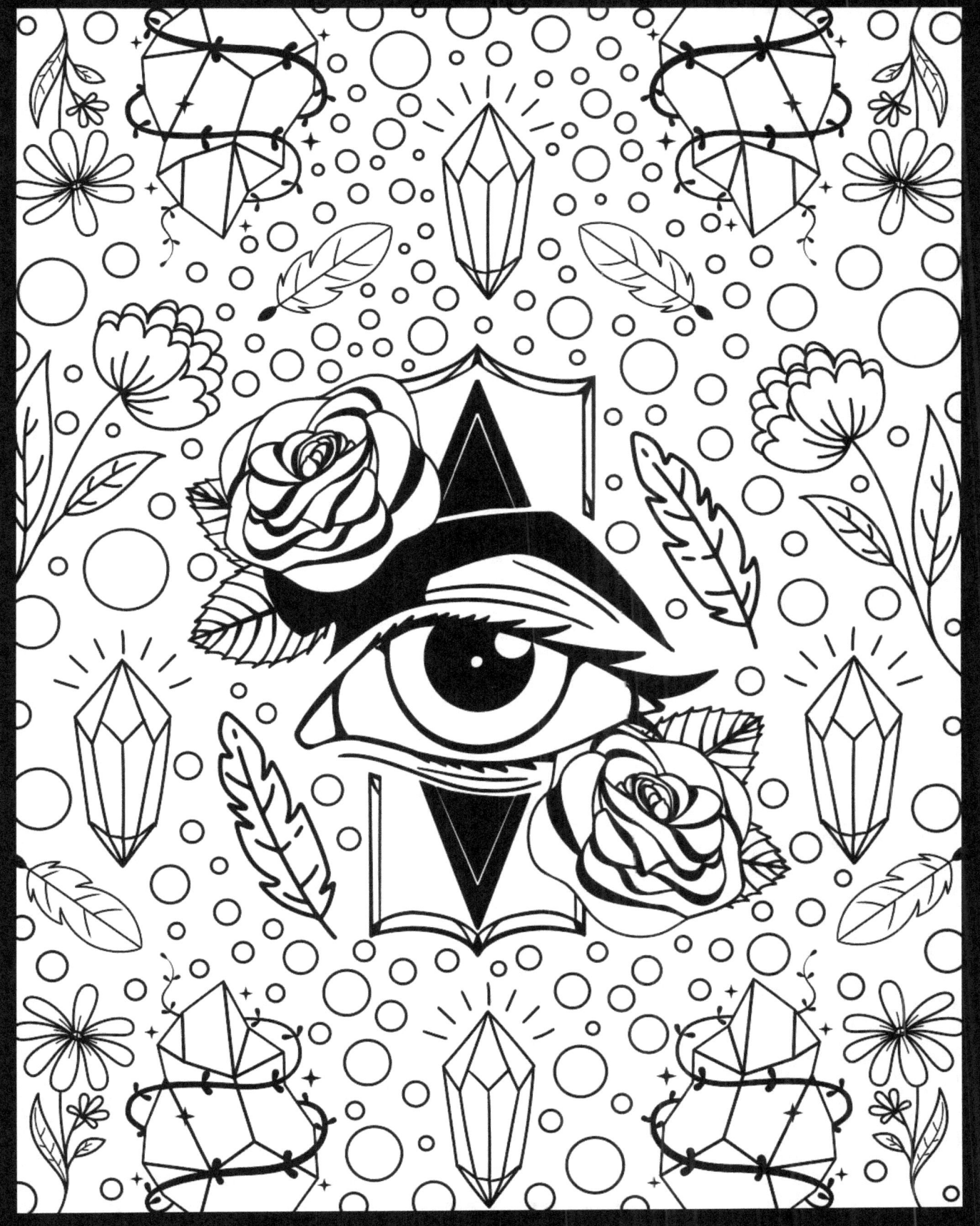

PROTECTION

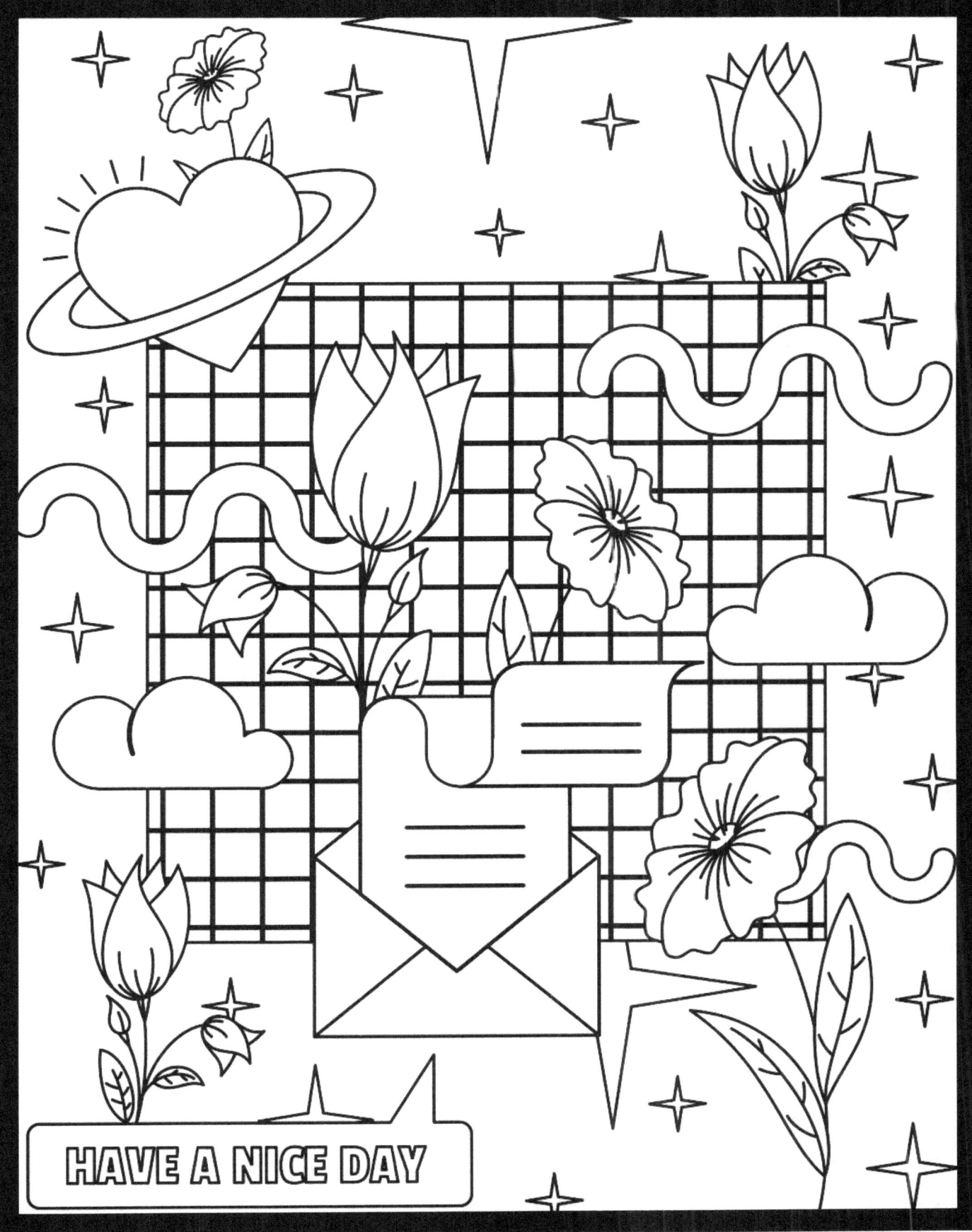

HAVE A NICE DAY

MESSAGES

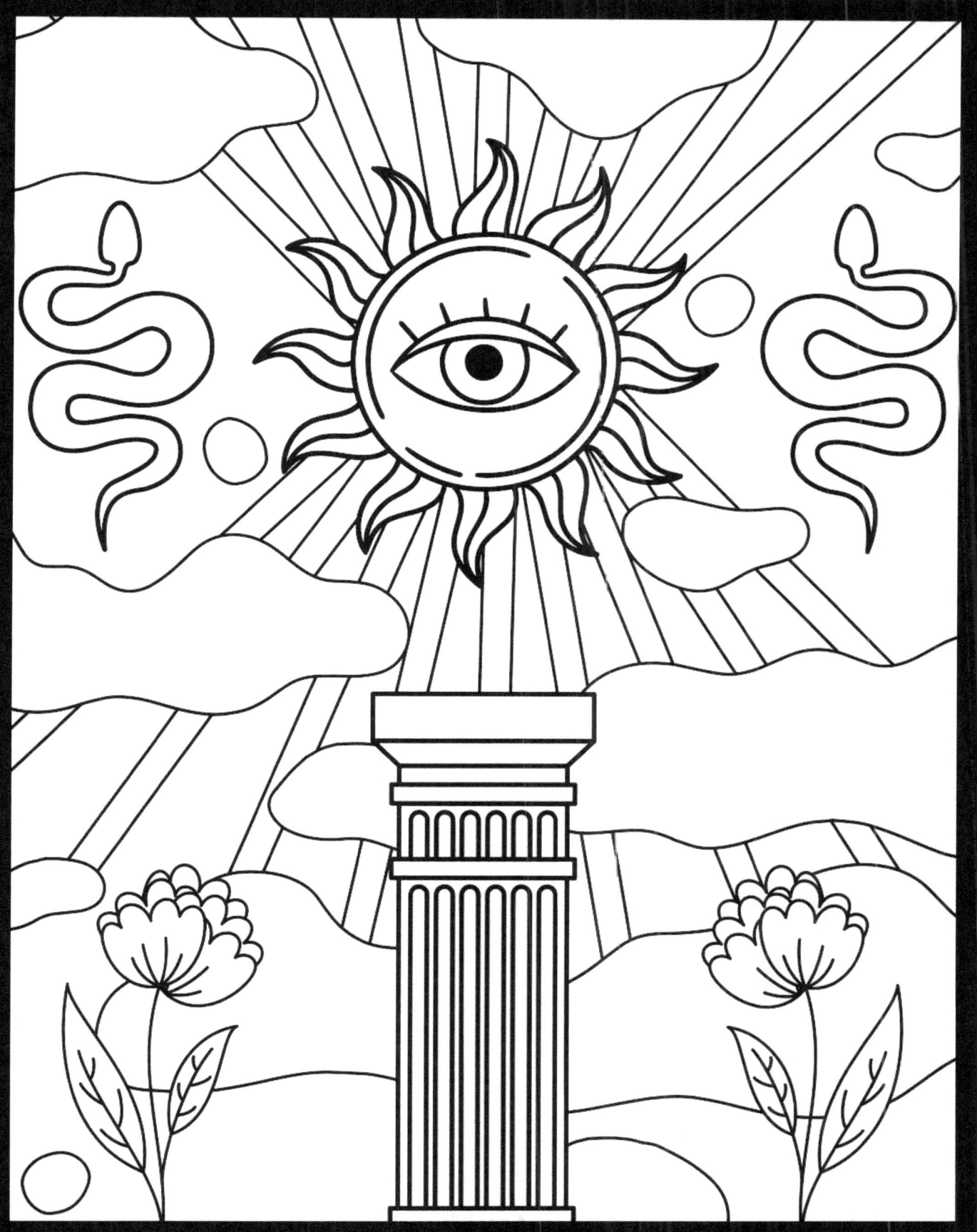

SUNSNAKES

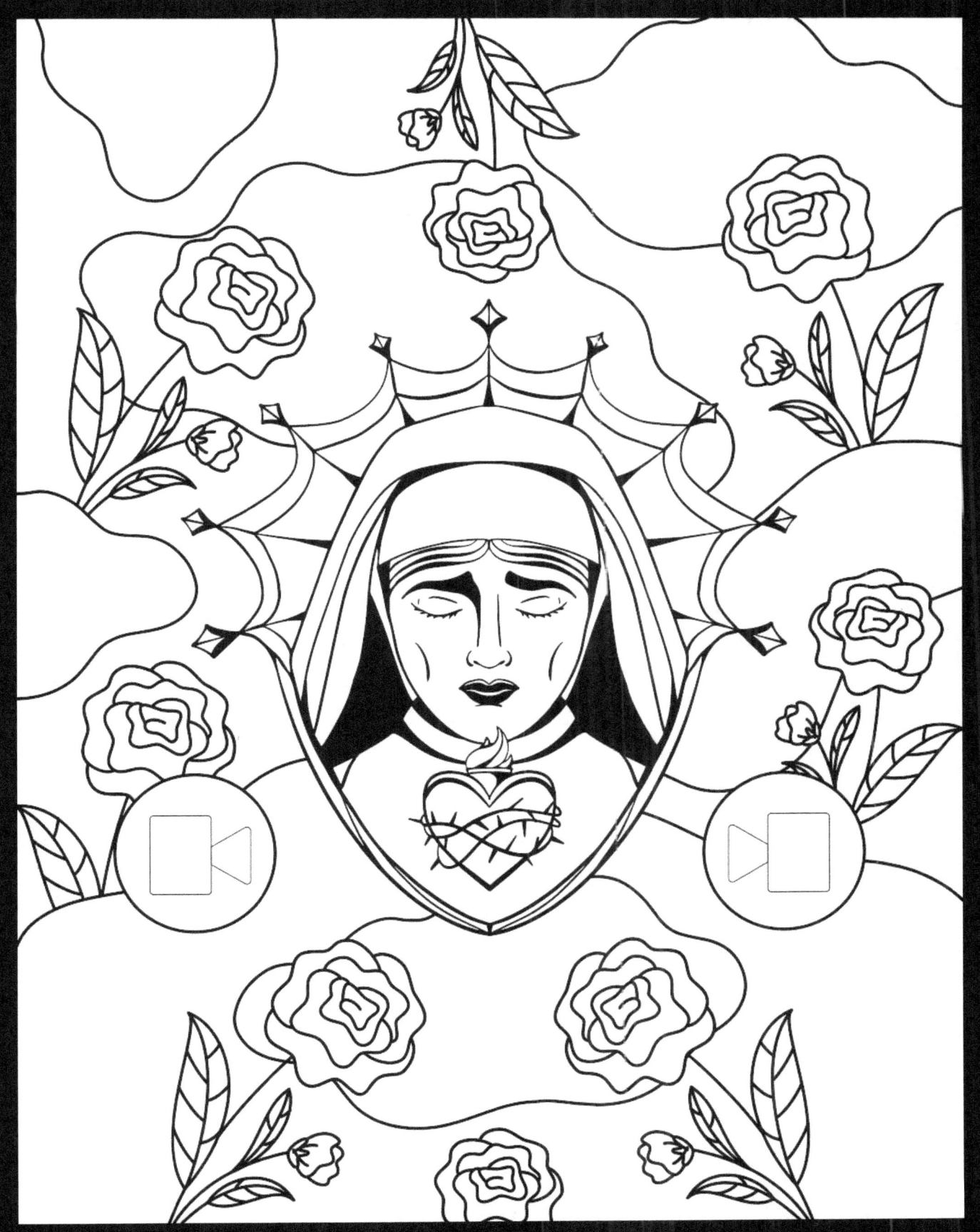

PLAY IT BACK

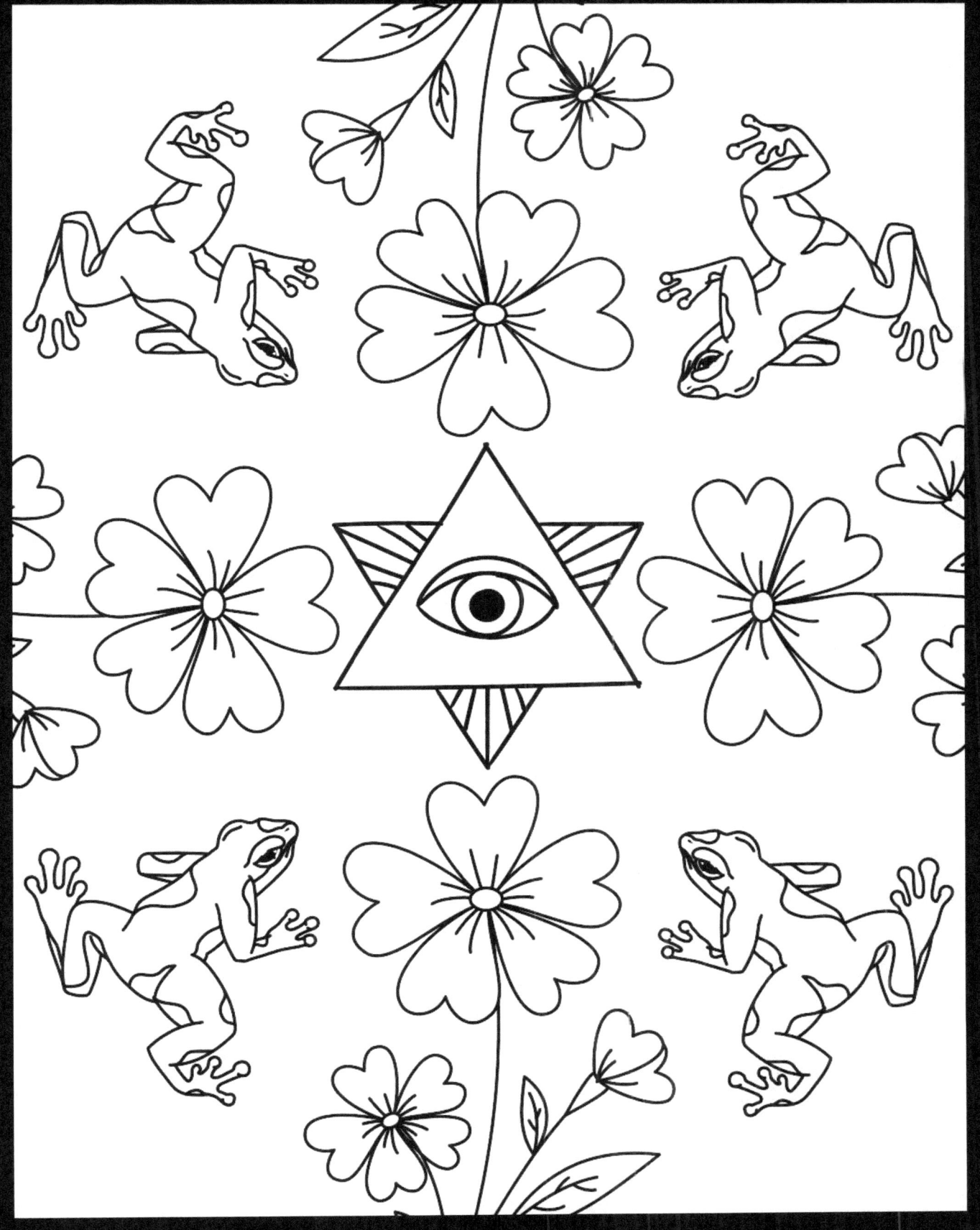

FOUR FROGS

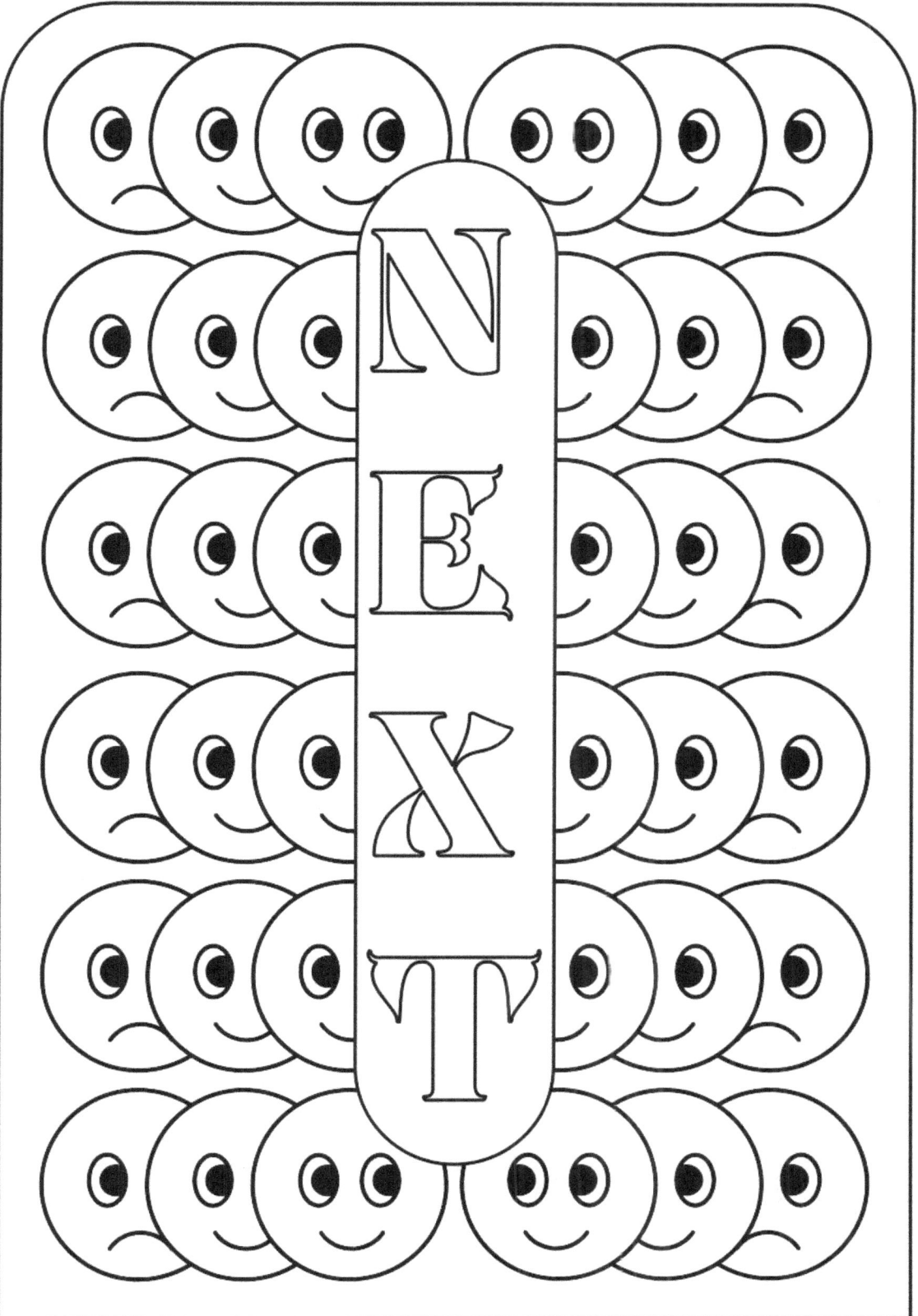

NEXT

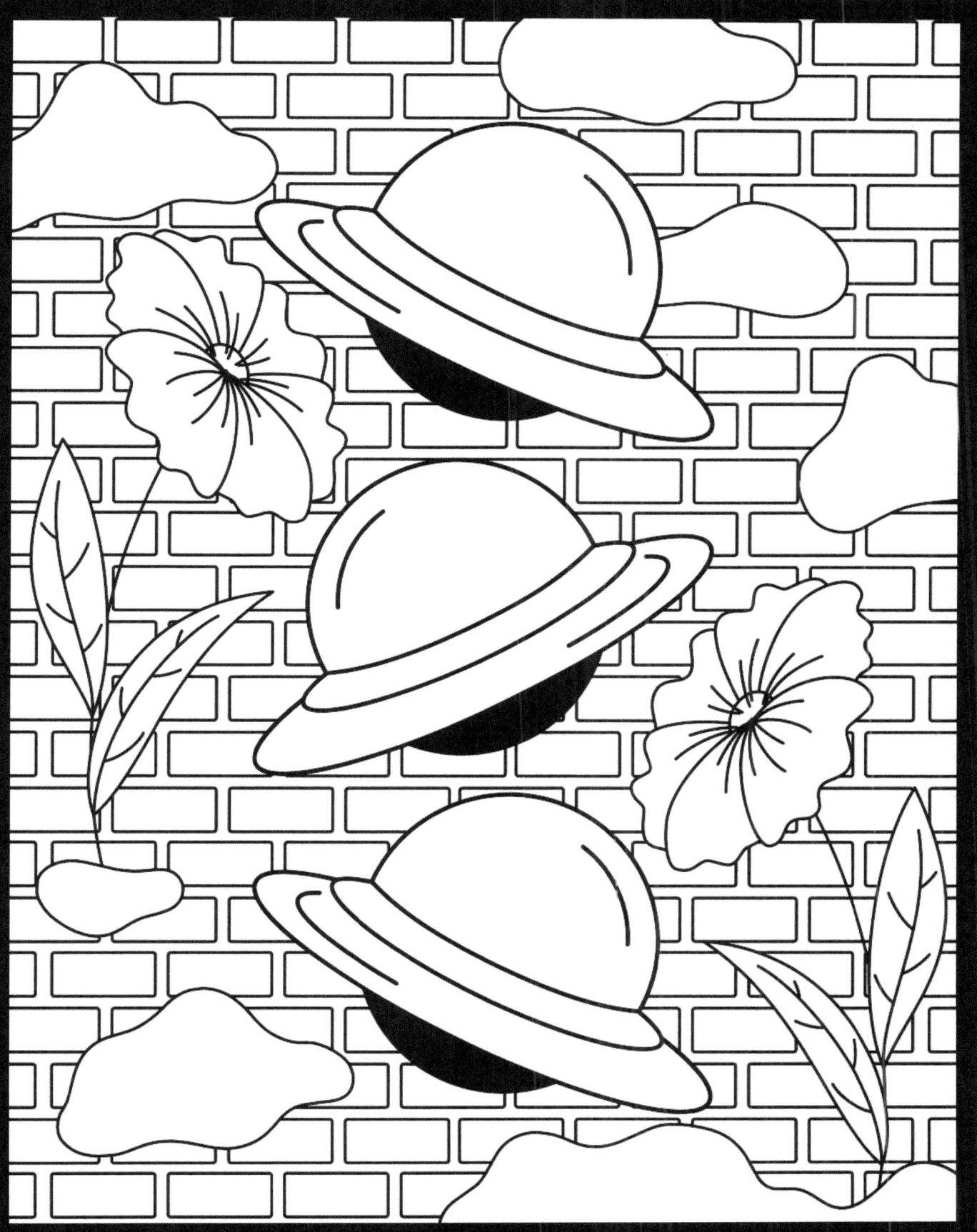

THREE SHIPS

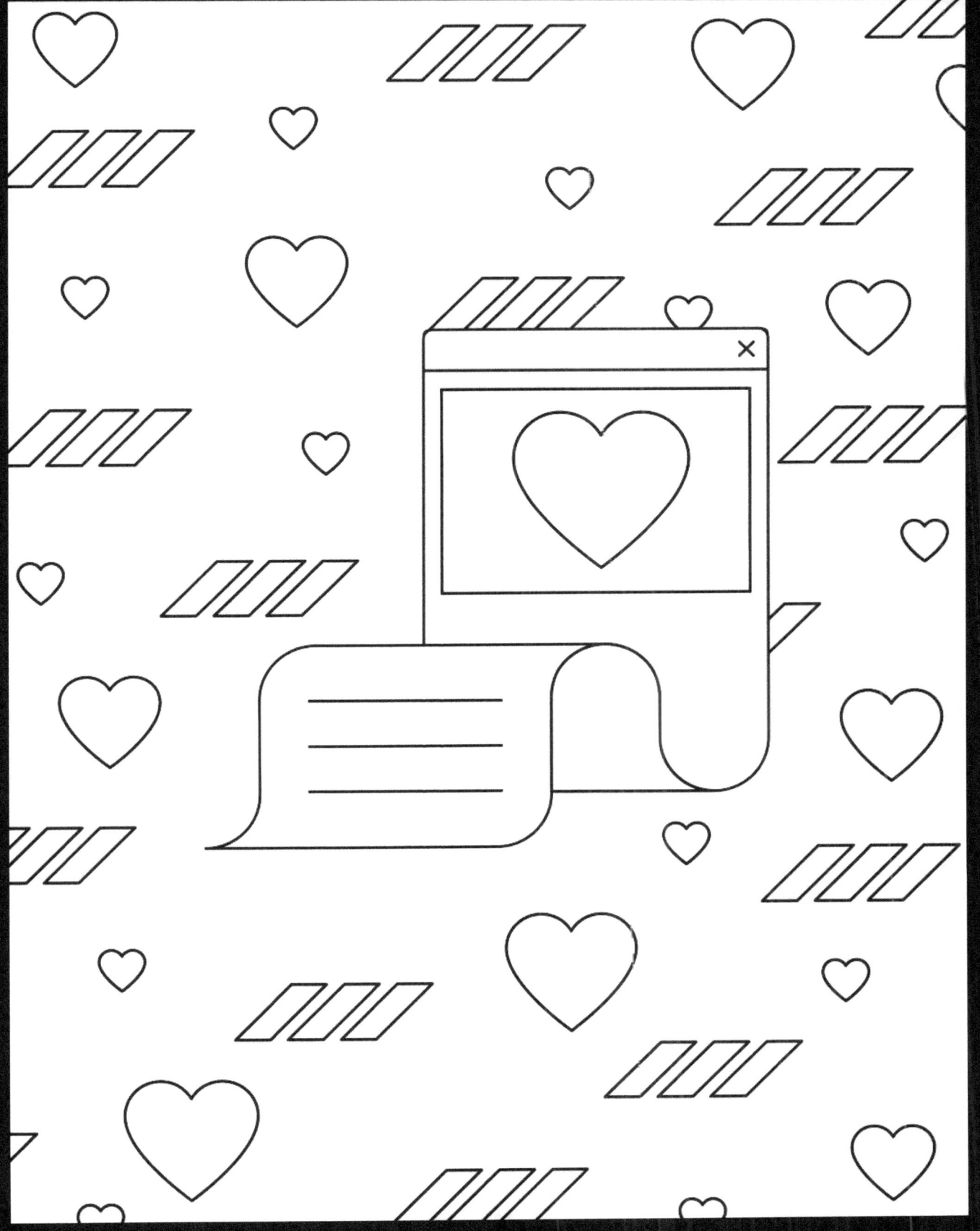

LOVE SCROLL

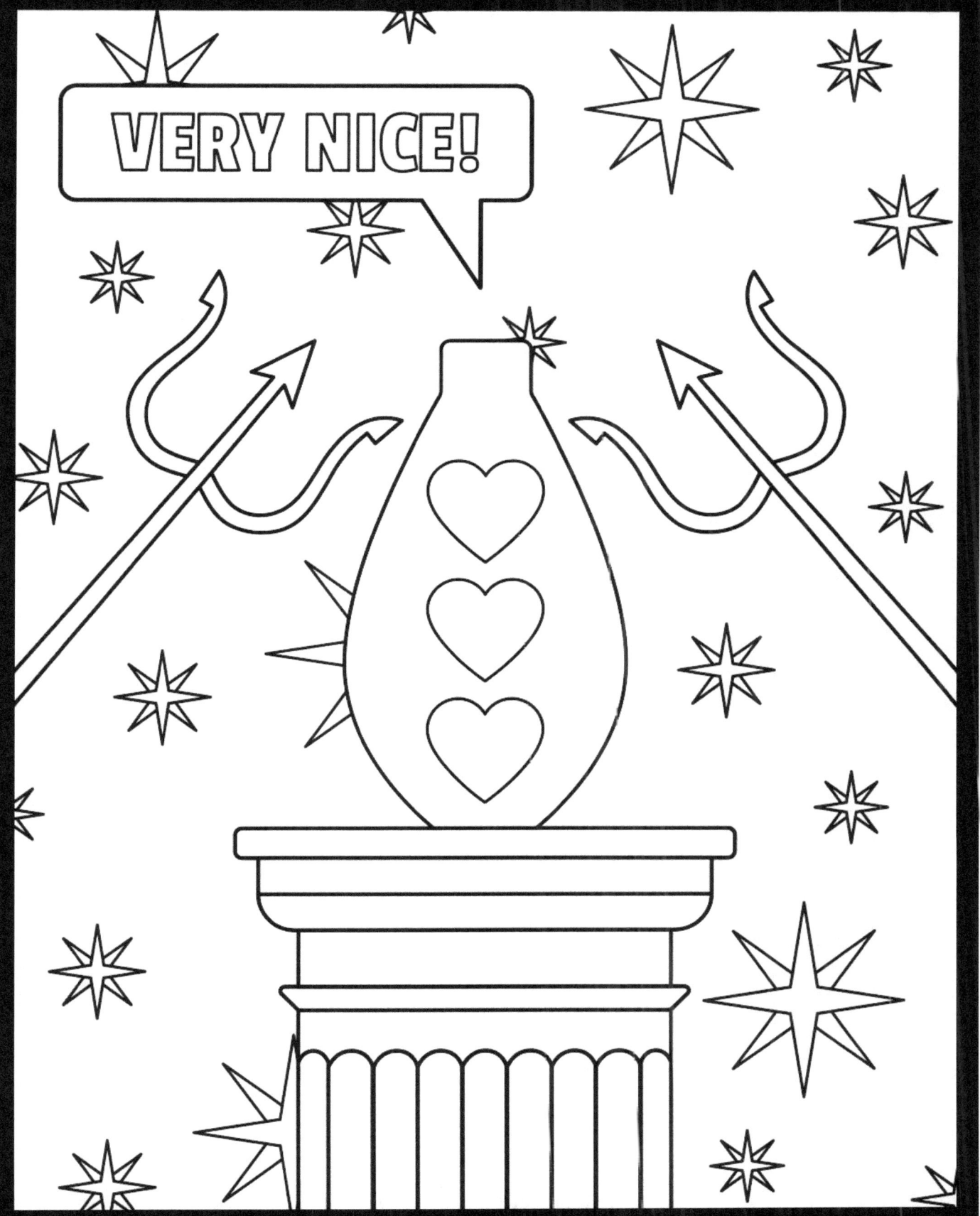

NICE VASE

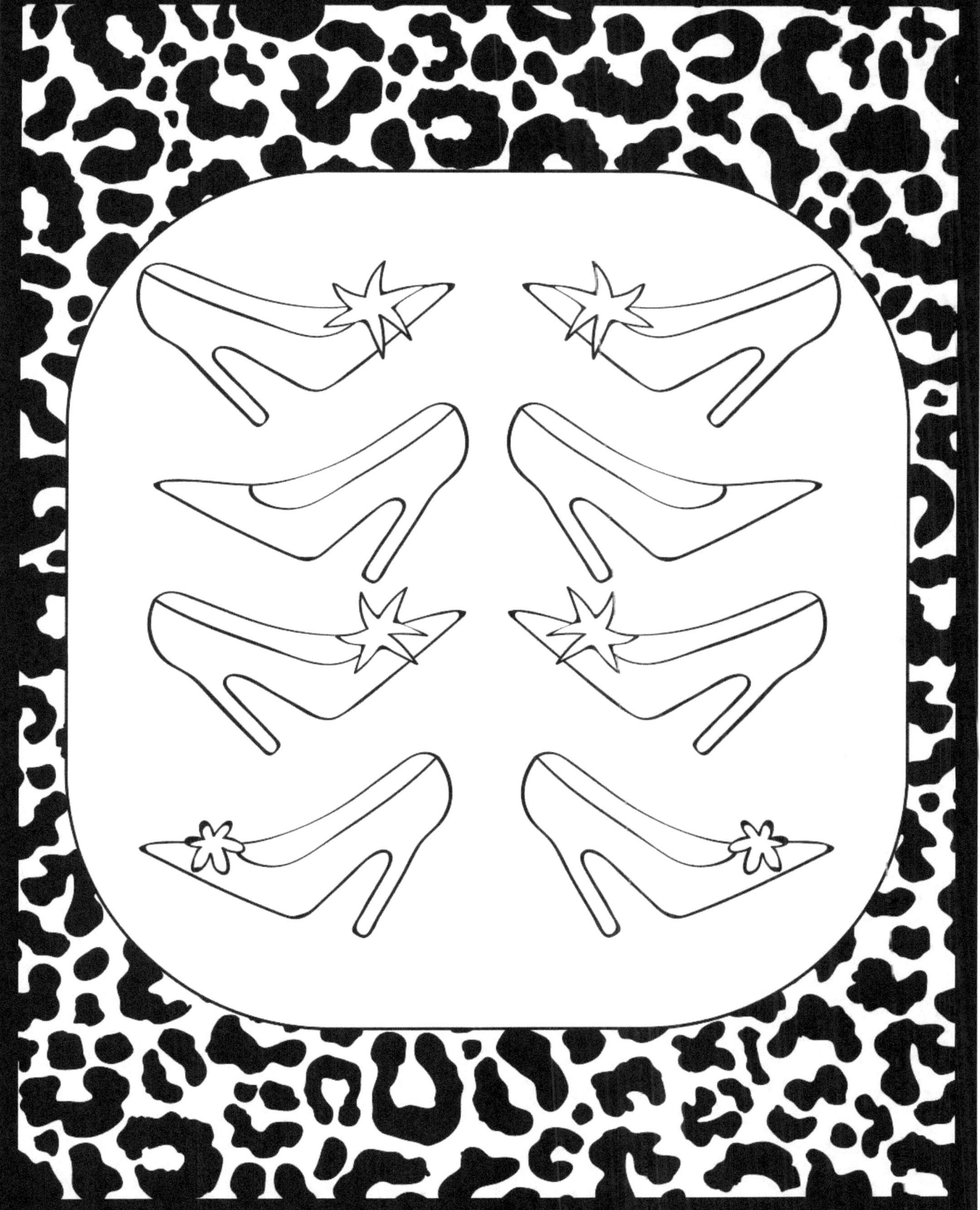

FABULOUS SHOES

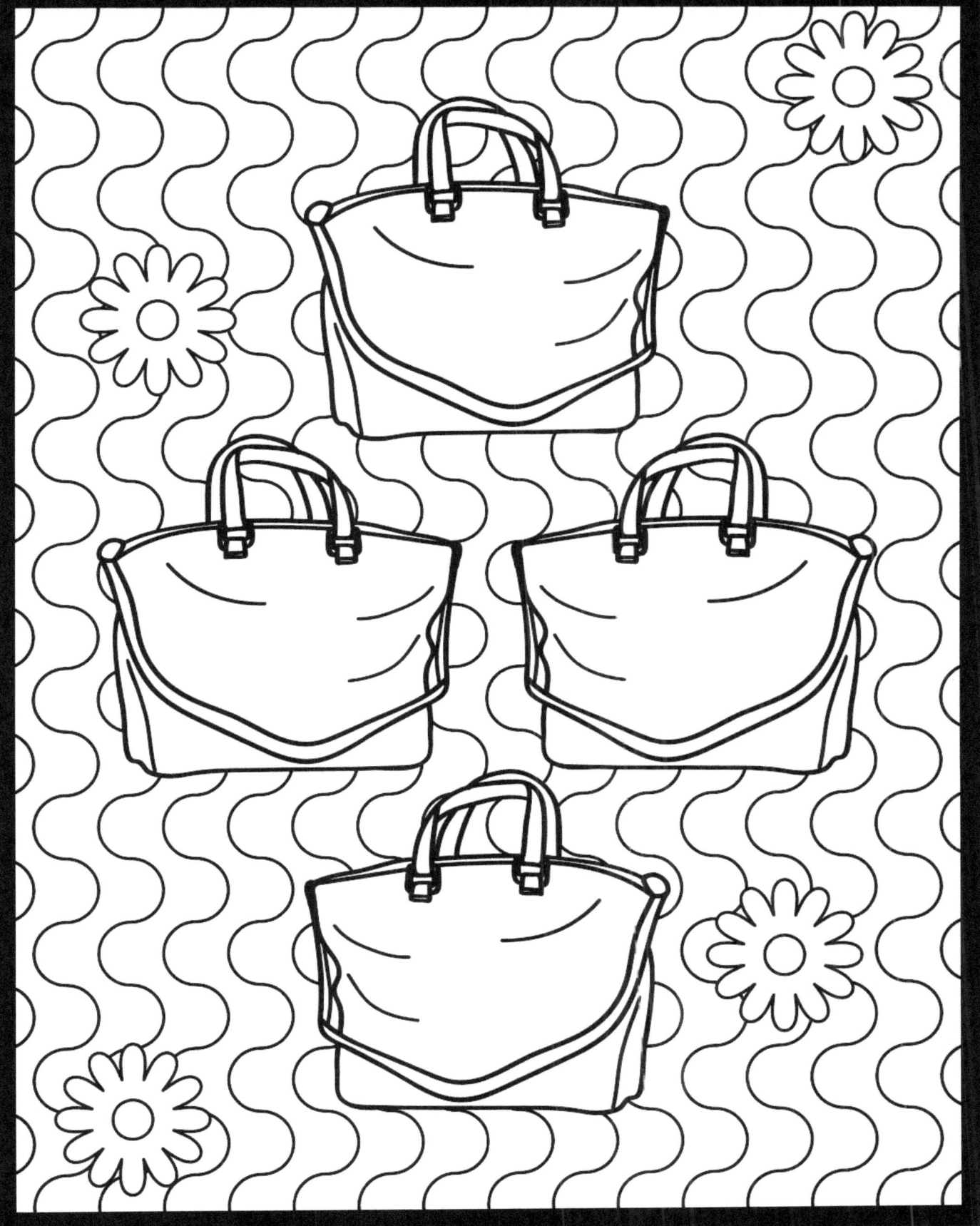

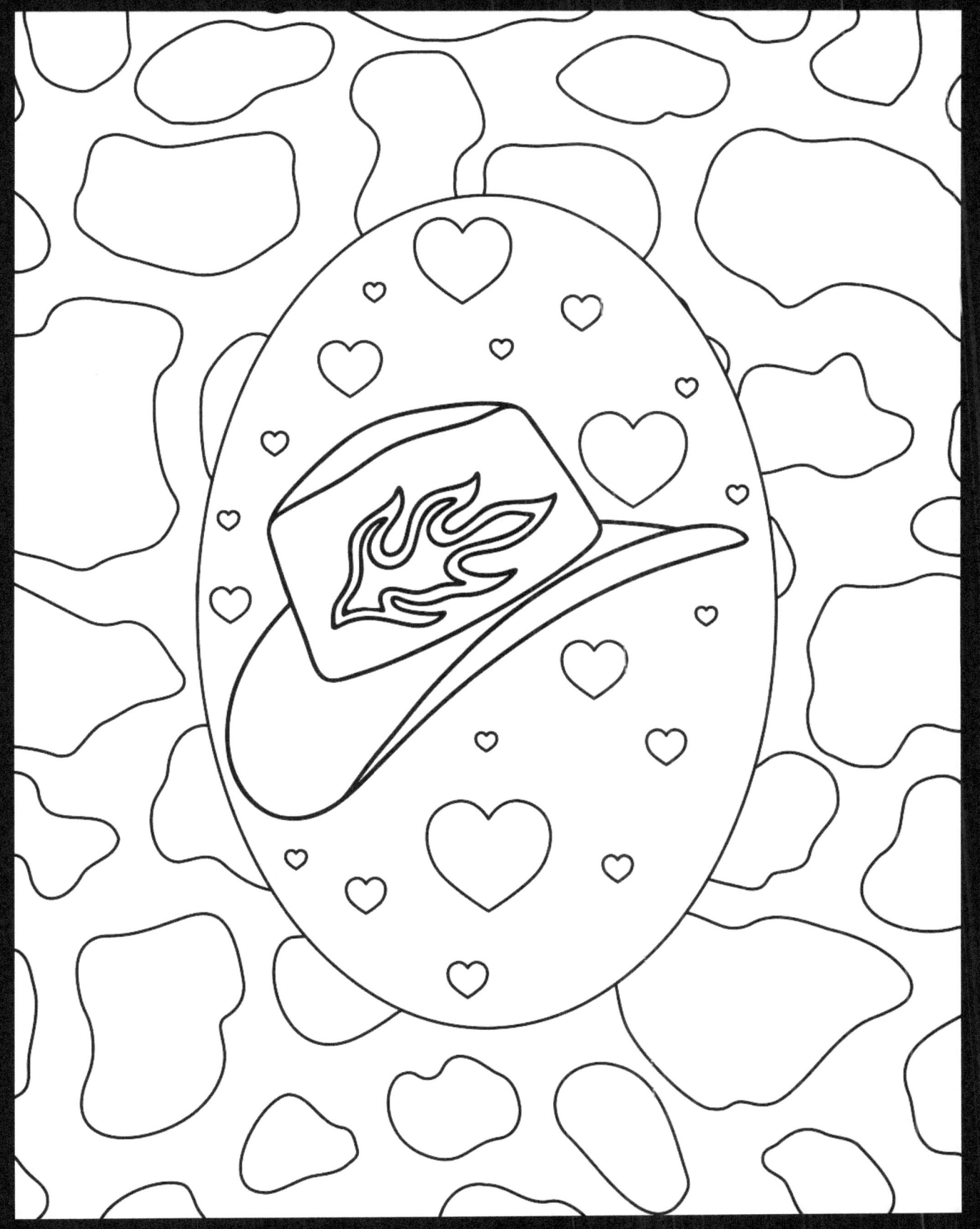

READY TO PARTY

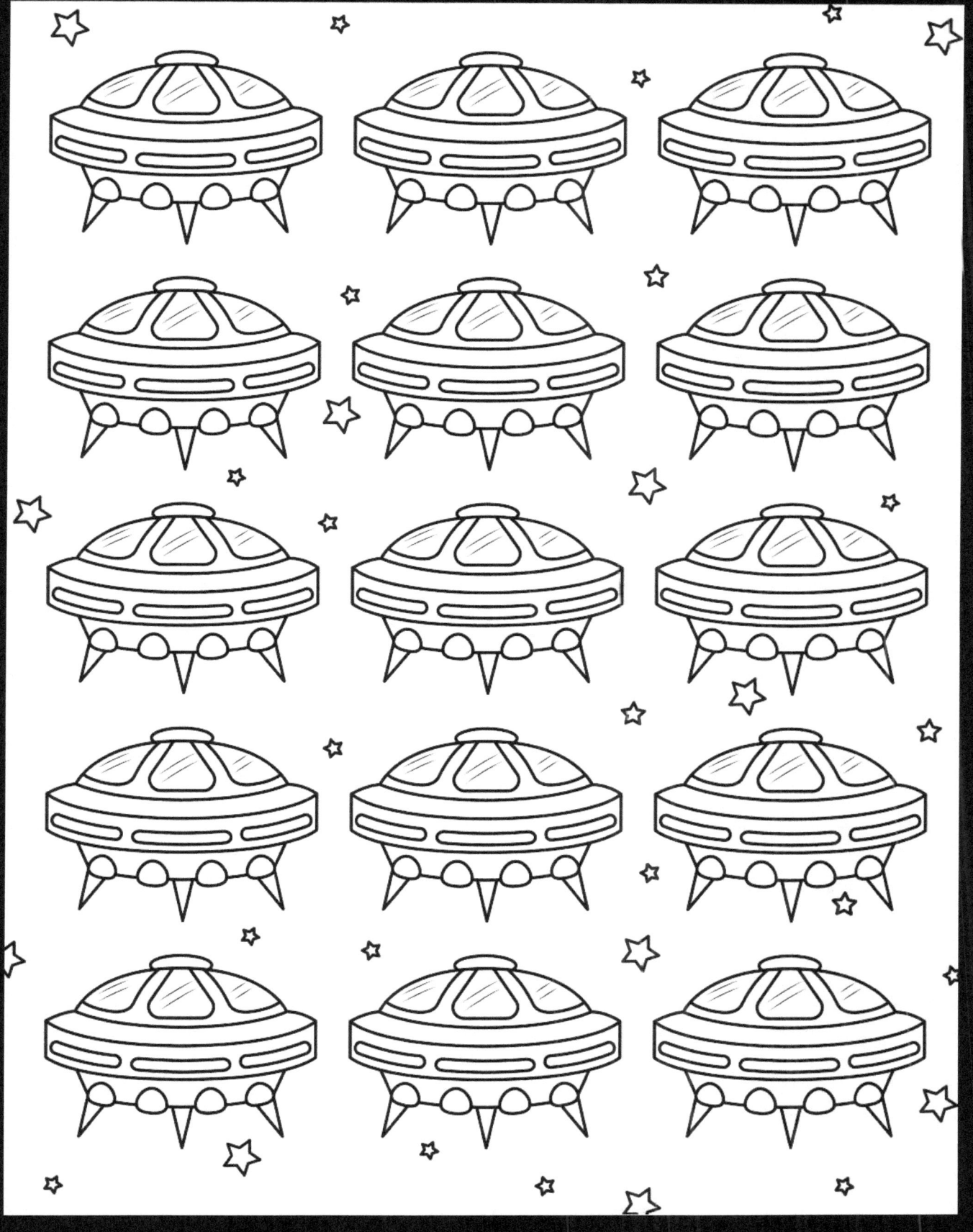

I AM OUT OF HERE

COLLECT THEM ALL!

MORE BOOKS FROM

AMNODE

90S WAVE
DESERT DREAMS
HAUNTED HALLOWEEN
FRESH TO DEATH
METAMORPHOSIS
SPOOKSHOW
TRANSCENDENTAL TAROT
SUPERNATURAL SPLENDORS
SPACE JUNK
AWAKENING
LOVE SPELL
ETHEREAL GARDEN
AS ABOVE SO BELOW
FEELING FABULOUS

THANK YOU

www.ingramcontent.com/pod-product-compliance
Lightning Source LLC
Chambersburg PA
CBHW082139290526
45794CB00008B/3095